PETER MAURIN

PETER MAURIN

Apostle to the World

Dorothy Day
with Francis J. Sicius

ORBIS BOOKS

Maryknoll, New York 10545

Founded in 1970, Orbis Books endeavors to publish works that enlighten the mind, nourish the spirit, and challenge the conscience. The publishing arm of the Maryknoll Fathers and Brothers, Orbis seeks to explore the global dimensions of the Christian faith and mission, to invite dialogue with diverse cultures and religious traditions, and to serve the cause of reconciliation and peace. The books published reflect the views of their authors and do not represent the official position of the Maryknoll Society. To learn more about Maryknoll and Orbis Books, please visit our website at www.maryknoll.org.

Library of Congress Cataloguing-in-Publication Data

Day, Dorothy, 1897-1980.
    Peter Maurin : apostle to the world / Dorothy Day ; with Francis J. Sicius.
      p. cm.
    ISBN 1-57075-550-7 (pbk.)
    1. Maurin, Peter. 2. Catholics—United States—Biography. 3. Catholic Worker Movement—History. I. Sicius, Francis J. II. Title.
BX4705.M4563D39   2004
282'.092—dc22

                        2004008349

I am a peasant. I have roots.

Peter Maurin

߷

*Dedicated to
the memory of
William D. Miller
friend and mentor*

*and to my wife
Isabel Valenzuela*

*and my daughters
Laurie-Anna
Paulina
Lucia*

Contents

Preface

An article in *Commonweal* magazine once described Dorothy Day as the most significant, interesting, and influential person in the history of American Catholicism.[1] Through her newspaper, *The Catholic Worker,* and the soup kitchens, farms, and Catholic activist groups it inspired, Dorothy Day gave the American Catholic laity a voice they never had and brought life to the Church's social conscience. On the centenary of her birth Cardinal John O'Connor acknowledged the contributions of this remarkable woman by announcing that he planned to initiate her cause for canonization.

One of the ironies of this story (or perhaps not if one thinks of the early careers of St. Francis or St. Augustine) is that this nominee for sainthood was in some respects far from "saintly." The daughter of a middle-class Protestant family, she spent her youth writing for socialist publications and became a companion of the likes of Max Eastman, Mike Gold, John Reed, and others among the literary left of the twenties. She had a number of affairs, an abortion, was married and divorced, all before the age of twenty-three. But then in her late twenties she had a spiritual experience that took her out of a common-law marriage and into the embrace of the Catholic Church.

In 1927 Dorothy Day found herself a single mother, living in New York's Lower East Side, and eking out a living writing articles in Catholic journals. The story may have ended there and Dorothy may have become a footnote in a book on Catholic women authors or female journalists, or some other little read monograph. But then she had a second "spiritual experience," which completed the job her initial conversion had begun. In

1932, she met Peter Maurin, a fifty-five-year-old French immigrant, who spoke English with a thick accent, and had some unique ideas about Catholic social reform.

Aside from their Catholic faith, the young woman and the grizzled street philosopher had nothing obvious in common, yet their fortuitous meeting radically altered the history of the American Catholic Church. It produced the spark that became the Catholic Worker, a movement which, over the next five decades, became the intellectual focal point for those who sought to raise a Catholic voice on issues of peace, human rights, and social justice. The humble office and soup kitchen of the Catholic Worker on New York's Lower East Side became a pilgrimage site for priests, nuns, and lay activists who came to discuss, examine, and absorb this new breath of spirit within the Church.

Articles, books, and even films, have documented the life of Day and marked her significance in the history of American Catholicism. And yet she continually eschewed this attention. "It was Peter," she insisted; it was his intellect and spirituality that motivated her and inspired the movement. But for most observers, Peter remained an inexplicable curiosity, and Dorothy's insistence on his significance was just another sign of her own deep humility.

Some listened to Dorothy and took her at her word. A few others in the early years of the movement were personally affected by Peter Maurin's intellect and sanctity. But they remained in the minority. And as time carried the movement further from its roots, the majority of Catholic Worker advocates and observers viewed Maurin as an eccentric, if visionary, figure, who recited banalities about Catholic social thought in his simple prose poems. Dorothy Day consistently disputed this dismissal of Maurin. Twelve years after their historic meeting she began to reflect on the powerful influence of this man on her own life and tried to put those thoughts on paper. Peter Maurin by that time had suffered a debilitating stroke. As Dorothy watched his slow but persistent deterioration, she began her biography. What she wrote provided the basis of this current work.

The way to begin this biography of the "gentle personalist" Peter Maurin is with the personal. Over ten years ago, I received a phone call from my friend and mentor, William Miller. In 1972, Miller had published the first scholarly attempt to measure the significance of the Catholic Worker movement in the context of American history. Following that work he went on to write the most definitive biography of Dorothy Day to date. He based both books on personal interviews with Day, as well as on her personal papers, which she had given him.[2]

He began the phone call to me that evening with none of the customary preliminary small talk and came straight to the point: "Do you think St. Thomas University would like to have my papers and notes on Dorothy and the Worker?" He had taught for two years at my university, and I think the way our little college muddled through its daily life amused him. No doubt our foibles offered a refreshingly humane contrast to the well-ordered, impersonal university life he had come to know through his entire teaching career. "Sure," I told him in the name of the university, without consulting anyone, though my instincts were correct.

I remember quite well the autumn drive with our library director, Margaret Elliston, to the old Bond plantation in Lloyd, Florida, the familial house of Bill's wife, Rhea, the home where he had written his first book on the Catholic Worker, twenty-five years prior. We spent a lovely weekend in the gracious hospitality of the Millers, and on Sunday afternoon we packed six boxes of notes into our rented car. While packing the last papers into the trunk, Bill looked at me and said quite sincerely, "You know, there are at least two or three books here." His words remained with me on the long drive south. The following Monday morning I put the papers in an eight-by-twelve-foot room, which serves as our archives. Margaret bought some archival boxes and over the next few months I did a preliminary organizing of the papers. Otherwise, there they sat for about two years.

Bill died a little over a year after this donation, and for the moment my own enthusiasm for working on them waned. Then during the summer of 1996 I participated in an NEH Summer Institute on Religious Diversity at Haverford College in Pennsylvania. During one session I spent some time talking about the Worker movement, Bill's papers, and the manner in which St. Thomas University had obtained them. When I finished one of the participants said, "I think you owe it to Bill to work on those papers."

The following September, when I returned to St. Thomas, I began to go through our new collection with renewed enthusiasm and in a more systematic manner. The majority consisted of notes Miller had taken from letters addressed to Day and the *Worker,* books contained in Peter Maurin's lengthy bibliography, and interviews with people important to the Worker movement. Also included were copies of Day's journals from the 1950s and '60s, which Bill's daughter Carol had typed from the originals. Among these typed manuscripts, I found one that especially intrigued me. It was simply called "Peter Maurin Biography by Dorothy Day." The condition of the paper and the type made it pretty obvious that this was Day's original work.

Up to that time, I had done very little research on Peter Maurin, so when I came upon this document I thought I had found something unique. When I asked Phil Runkel, the Catholic Worker archivist at Marquette University, about the Day manuscript on Maurin, he told me that he was aware of the document. He said some scholars had looked at the copy in the Marquette archives and concluded that most of it had already been published in the *Catholic Worker* and elsewhere. But I remained headstrong and convinced that I had a worthwhile project that might be edited and published. After reading the manuscript, however, I learned what an editor at Adair publishing house told her son-in-law, David Hennessy, in 1944:

"Dorothy Day has in my opinion not written a real biography of Peter Maurin here. The material is very sketchy, disorganized, and anything but a finished manuscript."[3]

After rereading the manuscript several times I understood why those who read it had dismissed it. It was, on first reading, as described: "sketchy, disorganized," and repetitive. Had the author been unknown I might have dismissed it as a poor imitation of William Faulkner. But unlike a Faulkner novel, there is only one voice repeating the story, Dorothy's, and she records her reflections from many perspectives. The various sides of Dorothy Day—activist, Catholic, writer, mother—reveal themselves in this short manuscript, but the personality trait most clearly revealed is the reflective, thoughtful Day. From her reflections we can begin to take a measure of the profound impact Maurin had on Day's spirituality and, in fact, on the life she chose for herself after 1933. This manuscript confirms the suspicion that had Peter Maurin not met Dorothy Day her spirituality would have remained merely personal. It was Maurin's profound influence that transformed the latent energy of Day's spirituality into the dynamic social force that became the Catholic Worker movement.

Although written somewhat unevenly, this document revealed a man of tremendous spiritual and intellectual strength. This apparently simple person gave Dorothy Day a vision of the infinite and provided a spiritual beacon that illuminated her own unique pilgrimage. It was this perspective that had been left out of other published accounts of Peter's life. Dorothy always paid homage to Peter as her mentor and teacher, but the general perception of Peter as an oddity, or at best an unorthodox philosopher, overshadowed the deep spirituality of the man. Arthur Sheehan, an early biographer of Maurin, had made the same observation. He complained that he had to leave much of the spiritual out of Peter's biography because his publisher felt that readers were more interested in the vignettes of his life, which emphasized his eccentricities.[4]

Marc Ellis, in a fine biography written in 1981, attempts to rescue Maurin from the confines of eccentricity by mining the verses that Dorothy called his "Easy Essays" for the gems of social philosophy hidden within. In Ellis's estimation Maurin was part of a diverse group of twentieth-century thinkers who comprised "an intellectual community of exile." Including such figures as Simone Weil, Martin Buber, Walter Benjamin, and Mahatma Gandhi, this community believed that a revival of the spiritual dimension of humanity was necessary to reverse the decline of civilization, a decline that began with the triumph of secularism in the eighteenth century. Ellis recognized Maurin as a type of what Simone Weil had called a "new saintliness"—one that would reject the political and economic alternatives of the day and "attempt to recover the personal aspects of social and private life to serve as witness to or advocate for the poor and finally to move beyond the political into a religious vision."[5]

Ellis places Maurin within a significant intellectual tradition in twentieth-century thought. But as Dorothy explains in her story of Maurin, his importance goes beyond that. All of Day's works are largely autobiographical, and this biography of Maurin is no exception. In writing this biography (which is also autobiographical) Day documents the profound spiritual influence of this man in whom, she writes, she saw "the face of God."

In editing this document I have attempted to resurrect Dorothy Day's impressions of Maurin and her reflections on his significance. The story she tells tends to ramble, so I have tried to play the role of narrator. In this role I have sought to keep Dorothy's voice on track without drowning it out, and to maintain a sense of historical context.

While on the subject of style I'd like to mention two important points. I chose to distinguish the two voices that are narrating this story through the use of two different fonts. For my own narrative I use a normal font, while Dorothy Day's words appear in italics. Also on the question of footnotes: the primary source for Dorothy's work is her manuscript, copies of which are located in both the Marquette Catholic Worker Archives and the St. Thomas University Miller/Catholic Worker Collection. I have not attempted to footnote the manuscript since it is itself a primary source of Day's own impressions, thoughts, and memories. I have documented my own comments, as well as the sources for additional excerpts from Dorothy's writing in *The Catholic Worker* and her other books.

The true author and inspiration for this work remains Dorothy Day, whom I met one time in 1972 on a visit to the Catholic Worker. I hitchhiked to New York City, got on a bus from Port Authority to Houston Street ("HOW STIN!" the driver shouted), and walked into St. Joseph House on East First Street. I went as a graduate student at work on a masters thesis on "Catholic Conscientious Objectors in World War II."

As I entered the storefront, someone asked if he could help me, and I mumbled quite self-consciously that I was there to see Dorothy Day. "Up the stairs, first door on your left," an indifferent voice blurted, and its owner continued working. I climbed the stairs, heard a typewriter, and wondered if I should interrupt.

"Don't bother her," I thought, and stood frozen in front of the door listening to the steady rhythm of thoughts flowing from mind to printed page. But another instinct overcame my fear, and I knocked on the door. Inside the room the typing stopped, a chair scraped across the floor, and the door opened. There she was, Dorothy Day! I don't really know in actuality if she was taller than me, but that day she certainly was. Apologetically I said something about being a graduate student interested in Catholic pacifists and World War II.

"Oh yes," she said, "Bill Miller's student. I'm very busy now but we can talk later, so go downstairs and ask Arthur Lacey for a broom. You can sweep the front sidewalk." This person whom I already held in awe grew even more. She saw that I was nervous and out of place, and with those few words she took all that away. She gave me a job that made me part of the community.

I'm not the first to be impressed by the sheer presence of

Dorothy Day. The distinguished Catholic writer John Cogley never forgot his first meeting with her, in 1936. "Although she had not achieved the spiritual authority that marked her later years," Cogley noted, "she was well on her way."[6]

The characteristics that left such a great impression on me, on John Cogley, and on thousands of others were not always part of Dorothy Day's demeanor. In the twenties, in Chicago, her literary friends at the Dill Pickle Club referred to her as "The Madonna of Oak Street Beach," and kidded her about playing the leading part in the film version of her autobiographical novel, *The Eleventh Virgin*.[7] In the late twenties Dorothy was a single mother, and a recent convert to Catholicism. She had a strong social conscience and a reputation as an activist. But, to her dismay, it was unclear how these various important facts of her life could be made to mesh. She remained especially uncertain about where her new-found religion would take her. She confessed this nervousness to publisher Llewelyn Jones. Writing from her beach house in 1927 she said, "You see I'm still religious, reading my missal faithfully, pinning medals on the baby, and going to mass." But in the same letter, she complained to Jones that despite her spiritual growth, "I guess I am still lacking."[8] Her faith was strong and her commitment to social justice held fast, but the inability to connect these two passions caused a chasm in her life, which she could not bridge. This reconciliation would not come until 1932, when Peter Maurin's pilgrimage brought him to her door.

INTRODUCTION

Day and Maurin

Peter Maurin is most truly the founder of the Catholic Worker movement. I would never have had an idea in my head about such work if it had not been for him. I was a journalist, I loved to write, but was far better at making criticism of the social order than of offering any constructive ideas in relation to it. Peter had a program, [and] I tried to follow it. . . . He opened our minds to great horizons, he gave us a vision.

—Dorothy Day[1]

Dorothy Day always acknowledged her spiritual and intellectual debt to Peter Maurin. When historian William Miller first suggested that he write her biography, she insisted that Peter ought to be the subject of his study. "Why don't you do a book on Peter?" she asked him, and offered him "boxes of material carefully arranged. . . . I would cooperate joyfully," she added."[2] Though Miller took the material, he used it to write the biography of Day, reasoning that the best way to get to Maurin was through her.[3] But Day was not pleased. "Why I have not awakened to the fact that you are doing my biography, not Peter's as I asked you, I do not know." But she relented. "I won't be bothered with this much longer," she wrote him. "Born in [18]97 I'll be eighty very soon."[4]

Day probably gave too much credit to Maurin. To assume that the movement came solely from his mind and energy would be to ascribe characteristics that simply were not his. Peter was an agitator and a motivator, not an organizer. His mission called him to awaken in people a vision of community that they might create with their own particular talents. Cyril Echele, an early Catholic Worker in St. Louis, remembered how Peter would speak of one's "mission." "You knew he had found his own mission. His joy of spirit would bubble over into his words." Urging people of like mind to join together, he would often say, "The next time you go to Seattle look up so and so. . . ." "He was a great contact man," Echele recalled.[5]

Some remembered Peter differently, leaving the impression that he was doctrinaire. Joe Breig, who wrote a fine article about him in *Commonweal* in the late thirties, helped create this image. "When Peter started talking," he wrote, "there was nothing to do but lean back and listen." Breig boasted that one night at a meeting he became the first person in history to quiet Maurin. "'Just a minute Peter,'" he repeated, "louder and louder until he closed his mouth. . . . 'What we've got to do is Christianize the world we're in,'" Breig argued, "'not try to go back to some world of the past.' There was a hushed pause," he recalled. "Then Peter pointed a rigid finger at [him] and said, 'Young man if that's what you think, that's your job. You do it!'"[6]

Dorothy viewed Peter differently. In him she saw "the most meek and submissive of men." She had "seen him again and again at meetings cut short by the chairman and with no sign of resentment, even when he has been stopped in the middle of a word. He [would] just say, 'Oh,' in a little apologetic tone and take his seat." Dorothy described him as being an "entirely unsuspicious" man who would "never think ill of anyone." On the contrary, she wrote, "He sees their good points to so extravagant an extent that . . . he has no judgment in regard to people. . . . How beautiful an attribute," she concluded, "always to see the good." Peter was not doctrinaire, she insisted, nor did he ever stifle someone's inherent passion or talent. On the contrary, Day recalled, "his encouragement sent many young men off on a career of writing and study, inspiring them to become propagandists and agitators for the Christian cause."[7]

When he first met Dorothy Day, Maurin did not say, "You will be a journalist and publish my ideas on Catholic social thought." Such a pronouncement would conflict with his anarchist spirit. He simply saw her talent for journalism and passion for social justice and helped her to order her life by putting these predilections at the service of Christianity. "You should start a paper," was not a command by Peter, merely recognition of Dorothy Day's abilities. As she later pointed out, "Undoubtedly it is proof of his genius that he left much for people to find out for themselves by their own reasoning. He leaped as if it were from crag to crag of thought expecting his listeners to fill in the gaps." Dorothy noted that Peter did not dictate, he simply "held before [people] a vision."[8]

Day explained that she decided to write his biography in order "to point to the nature of Peter's influence over [her]." She denied that the attraction was "physical, spiritual, or mental." At least "not in the usual sense of the word." Actually, at first meeting, the young journalist barely understood the grizzled, unkempt, fifty-five-year-old man. "I had a hard time connecting with him," she recalled, "as a peasant, a man, and a Frenchman." The early months were a struggle for both of them. "It was amazing," Day wrote in *The Long Loneliness,* how little we understood each other at first."[9] But, she pointed out, "he made you feel a sense of his mission as soon as you met him and he aroused in you a sense of your own capacities for work [and] for accomplishment."[10]

Maurin determined after their first meeting that in order to help her realize her mission Day would have to understand better the social message of the Church. In her manuscript on Peter she recalled the first books he brought her to read. "Besides Kropotkin, Fr. Vincent McNabb, and Eric Gill, there were Jacques Maritain, Léon Bloy, Charles Péguy, Don Luigi Sturzo, Karl Adam, [and Nicholas] Berdyaev. It was hard on us both," she recalled. "Many a time I listened and listened unwillingly. I could only go one step at a time."[11]

Maurin's style of teaching eventually began to intrigue her, however. "He never preached. He never talked about the spiritual life as he did the life of the world around him." She emphasized that he was a materialist, an "apostle to the world" of the poor and the worker, whom Dorothy professed to love and whose life she wished to share. Peter's Christianity was not simply spiritual, she noted, for it laid out a practical plan that reconciled the apparently fragmented design of her heart and mind. She immediately saw that Peter's view of a socially and economically responsible Christianity provided an alternative to society as envisioned by both industrial capitalism and Communism. His synthesis helped to remove a serious conflict, which had troubled Dorothy since her conversion.

Dorothy was anticapitalist and her new Church was strongly anti-Communist. Yet Communism, she wrote, had provided the new torch that set the world afire.[12] Because of her conversion to Catholicism, she felt she had to venture carefully into areas where she had previously treaded fearlessly. The Christianity that she knew from her conversion had been made safe for the capitalists. She had learned nothing of the "social dynamite of the church," Peter told her, because scholars had been sitting on it for centuries.[13]

"Peter's great mission," Dorothy wrote, "was to bring back the communal aspects of Christianity, to rescue the communal from Communism." Maurin believed that the Church was right in attacking the "heresy" of Communism, but it was wrong in simply attacking the heresy and not addressing the cause. People fall into heresy, he explained, when the Church neglects or ignores one aspect of the truth. The "heresy" of Communism had emerged because the Church had not embraced the message of social responsibility inherent in the Gospels. Maurin's vision of a socially dynamic Church fit Day's disposition and helped her create a mission for herself. The obvious fact that Peter lived his philosophy also affected Dorothy profoundly. He had taken his theories of voluntary poverty and of Christian love and put them into practice. Soon Dorothy created the newspaper Peter had suggested, or at least a reasonable facsimile thereof, and thus she began to present Peter's ideas to the world.

In *The Catholic Worker* she introduced not only Peter's life and ideas, but also her own vision (which he had inspired) of a dynamic social Christianity. Dorothy especially liked the idea that Peter was a worker. Describing him, she wrote: "He looks as though he were rooted to the ground, gnarled, strong, weather-beaten. He reminds me of a tree trunk, of a rock. His shoulders are broad, he has a chest like a barrel, his head is square and so is his face. Down at the Easton farming commune," she wrote, "he likes to break rocks to mend the road, [and] dig ditches to pipe the water from the spring."[14] Inherent in her description is an important message for the poor. This man who is writing these truths of Christianity in the *Catholic Worker* is not a bishop or a university professor. Our founder is one with you, she told her readers. "He is a simple man who wears worker's shoes that he buys on the Bowery for three dollars, [who] wears heavy underwear [and who] washes out the cuffs and the collar of his blue work shirt, dries it overnight, and puts it on again unironed."[15] Peter dignified the poor, calling them "ambassadors of God." Very few of the poor whom Dorothy encountered possessed the dignity and demeanor of Peter Maurin, but she continued to see Peter in all of them.

Peter became so immersed in his mission that outer appearances or his personal material condition meant little to him. In this state, he became a special focus for Dorothy's universal concern for the poor and downtrodden. In her biography of him she wrote, "I've seen him setting out [with ashes all over him from tending the fire] to give a lecture somewhere all unbrushed and uncombed and have run after him to refurbish him a bit for company. It's for the sake of the others, I tell him."[16]

One very cold February morning she asked Peter if he was

warm enough. "No," he answered matter-of-factly. And Dorothy went right away to correct the problem. It angered her to learn that someone had taken his blankets and that he was sleeping in his clothes, under his overcoat, and leaving the oil burner going all night to keep warm.[17]

Although she cared for many of his material needs, Dorothy found many of Peter's habits disconcerting. For example, manners were not important to Peter. She noticed "he would precede others through the door, forget to take off his hat, not give up his seat to an old woman unless he was told, nor say thank you when given anything. He was unconscious of the need for such courtesies. To Peter," Dorothy Day observed, "a gentleman was one who did not live off of the sweat of someone else's brow."[18] His profligacy with money also bothered Day. She once wrote to a priest that Peter would be very glad to come up and spend a week with him. But she pleaded, "When you send his fare be sure and send him a return ticket to New York; if you give him the money he is liable to spend it and go someplace else. As you mention making him an offering," she continued, "I also ask you not to give him that but send it to the Catholic Worker—if you give it to him he might decide to visit Bishop O'Hara in Montana or some equally distant place as he is very impulsive."[19]

Peter's puns and other eccentricities in his writing also bothered Day. Speaking English as a second language, Peter saw rhythms and peculiarities in words that would not occur to a native speaker, and they amused him. He liked to share these oddities with his listeners. He wanted to make the "papal encyclicals click," he would say; people bought "stocks till they got stuck." He was proud of his clever verbal gymnastics, though they caused the writer Day to shudder. But this became for Day another lesson from the man who lived his vision. "His puns and paradoxes used to make me blush," she confessed, "but they were as much a part of Peter as his clothes." She soon realized that her "intellectual disdain was almost as bad as snobbish disdain of those who made fun of Peter's clothes or appearance, or the clothes and appearance of anyone for that matter."[20]

Marquette University Archives

Against those who attacked Peter for his appearance, Dorothy defended him strongly, as she would any of the poor. She particularly objected to those who called him a bum. "Peter gave his labor," she pointed out, "where it was needed [and] earned his living with the sweat of his brow. We saw how he could work at manual labor on our farms." In later years, "Peter was to speak at seminaries and colleges. But he never received more than modest offerings," she observed, "or his fare paid from place to place."

Dorothy's complaint may well have been that of any of the exploited working poor. "If he had worn a dress suit, carried a suitcase, stayed at a good hotel," she noted, "the offerings would have turned into fees, and the respect accorded him would have been greater."[21] "I write these things not with bitterness," Day stated, "but to make the point that Peter often made, that poverty should be respected, that we should see Christ in every man regardless of his clothes." Dorothy "thanked God" that "Peter's intelligence and sanctity were apparent to many, in spite of clothes. His old suit cast off of someone else, his dollar suitcase full of books and pamphlets, his bearing, his radiant, serene face, these," she noted, "all came to be loved in many a circle around the country."[22]

Peter's faith, which meshed so completely with his life, affirmed all of Dorothy's spiritual inclinations. Solidarity with the poor remained at the core of Peter's message. Dorothy knew this was what set him apart, what distinguished him from other great contemporary teachers and philosophers. Dorothy Day may or may not have known of Antonio Gramsci, the Italian Marxist philosopher, but she recognized in Peter what Gramsci described as an "organic intellectual," one who does not simply partake in eloquent oratory, "but who remains in contact with the source of the problems he sets out to resolve."[23] At some point in his life, around the age of fifty, Maurin underwent a profound conversion. Ideas he had been working out all his adult life took on a new reality for him. He came to the conclusion that he must live as he believed and that if there were to be a revolution of values it must begin with him. He believed that everyone had the potential to realize goodness, and through the example of his own life he believed that he would exhort others to follow their best instincts.

Among other things, he came to believe that working for wages was wrong, so he stopped working for wages. In an age that glorified the rugged individual, he advocated community. In a system that measured success in terms of material goods, he owned nothing. Rejecting the bourgeois concept of the nuclear family, he sought his family among kindred spirits, including simple workers, panhandlers, investment bankers, and university professors.

"In a time when we are living in an acquisitive society,"

Dorothy observed, "Peter Maurin is the poor man. Perhaps that is what makes Peter so important a person, this tremendous faith he had not only in God but also in man. He was an apostle to the world," she wrote. "It is this which sets him apart from other men, from other saints of the Church of God who went around preaching penance, reminding men of their relationship with God and eternity."

Peter's very being was a demonstration of his faith. "Peter," Dorothy observed, "thought not only in terms of eternity, but of the present life where we are actors, where we are placed as though on a testing ground, to prove ourselves for eternal life." Dorothy recognized the unique genius of Maurin. His life represented a cohesive intellectual, spiritual, and practical synthesis, which stood as a positive alternative to the rapidly unraveling philosophic fabric of the Enlightenment. He represented the very order of spirit, intellect, and action that Dorothy had been seeking all her life. It took a while, but she soon realized that this man held a special truth and a spiritual sense that she had not found in other sources of her new religion. Dorothy was stubborn, questioning, and skeptical, certainly a difficult student, but once she understood the significance of Peter's message she dedicated herself to understanding and living the ideal that he presented.

Dorothy observed a religious foundation to whatever Peter discussed, be it philosophy, history, sociology, or economics. But at the same time none of his thought was ethereal, it all had to do "with the world and this life which we know and love and with the needs of our bodies for food, clothing and shelter." Peter provided for Dorothy Day the connection between the eternal and the finite. "The dignity of the worker. The dignity of work. The goodness of God's goods. Man as co-creator. These were the things he believed in," Dorothy observed. "He had faith in himself, in his own importance as a lay apostle, and that faith was sufficient for him to rise above any and all rebuffs from whatever source they came." She admired his confidence in the message he presented. "It was inconceivable to Peter," she noted, "that anyone should be uninterested [in his program]. That is part of the secret to his success. He had a gentle insistence, an enthusiastic generosity, and an assumption that one was intellectually capable of grasping the most profound truths and was honestly ready to change one's life to conform thereby." [24]

Peter's life reminded Dorothy of the first letter of St. John in the New Testament. In this letter John discusses seeing the face of God in our love for one another. John wrote, "No man hath seen God at any time. If we love one another, God abides in us; and His charity is perfected in us. If any man say I love God and hates his brother he is a liar. For he that loves not his brother whom he sees, how can he love God whom he sees not?"

Peter profoundly influenced Dorothy Day because he made the Gospels come alive through his every action. "When people come into contact with Peter Maurin," she wrote, "they change, they awaken, they begin to see, things become as new, they look at life in the light of the Gospels. They admit the truth he possesses and lives by, and though they themselves fail to go the whole way, their faces are turned at least toward the light. And Peter was patient," she observed. "Looking at things as he did in the light of history, taking the long view, he was content to play his part, to live by his principles, and to wait." He always reminded her of "the necessity of the long view, of the vision." He taught her to see all things in the light of eternity. Dorothy felt that it was this "longer view that connected them to the infinite and made the work of the day, what [they] did here and now so important that each thought, each decision, each step [they] took determined the future, not only for themselves but for the world."

Dorothy believed that "Peter was so conscious of the overwhelming fact that he was a child of God, and an heir to heaven, that he made others feel it." His actions and words often reminded her that we are all partakers of divine life. As Peter frequently told her, "The Christ life was in all of us." Maybe it was, she admitted, "but not as [much] as it was in Peter."[25] He taught her "the joy and life-giving qualities of the works of mercy." "He has brought Christ to us in the face of the poor," Dorothy observed, "as surely as the Blessed Mother brought Christ to Elizabeth." She concluded, "He has shown us the way, with his poverty and his works of mercy, and that way is Christ."[26] From Peter she learned how to create a model of eternal community in time.

"Without him," Dorothy concluded, "I would never have been able to find a way of working that would have satisfied my conscience. Peter's arrival changed everything, I finally found a purpose in my life and the teacher I needed." Dorothy Day's biographers concur that she constantly sought the truth. But for Day, truth had to be reconciled with her intellect, her spirituality, and the real world around her. When she was thirty years old she felt she found this unity of thought, spirit, and action in the Catholic Church, but as her own letters and autobiography tell us, she was often frustrated in her new-found religion. Not until she met Maurin did the restlessness end. With his inspiration she founded the Catholic Worker movement where, as she tells us, her longing was fulfilled. It is absolutely certain that without Dorothy Day there would have been no Catholic Worker, but it is also certain that without the spiritual influence of Peter Maurin, there would not have been a Dorothy Day with the perspective capable of creating that movement. Dorothy Day acknowledged this. She had no doubt of Peter Maurin's spirituality, and she knew that the divine life existed within him.[27]

Breadline on Mott St.

1

The French Peasant

⤳

People who built the Cathedral of Chartres
knew how to combine
cult, that is to say liturgy,
with culture, that is to say philosophy,
and cultivation, that is to say agriculture.
                                        —Peter Maurin

All of Dorothy Day's work is in part autobiographical, and that includes her biography of Peter Maurin. When she completed this narrative in 1947 Maurin had recently suffered a stroke, which accelerated his physical decline. He was no longer the energetic agitator who had inspired her to begin the Catholic Worker in 1932. Perhaps as he neared his end, Day ruminated on how her life had changed as a result of meeting this strange Frenchman, and perhaps these reflections provided the motivation for this biography. Certainly her introduction suggests this. For instead of beginning in a traditional style of describing time, place, background, and historic context of her subject's birth, Day created a journalistic picture of the place where Maurin was concluding his life. In reality it was a space of her design, not his. Nevertheless in this introduction she provided an intriguing and picturesque portrait of the Lower East Side of New York in the mid-1940s.

Mott Street is a mile long, extending from Houston Street down to Chatham Square. It is a curved street, very slightly and gently curved. It turns into Chatham Square where the Bowery becomes Park Row, and where East Broadway, New Bowery, the Bowery, Park Row, and Mott Street all run together. All of Chatham Square is dark and dank under the elevated lines, for here the Second Avenue line branches out and goes down Park Row to the Brooklyn Bridge and down New Bowery to South Ferry, a mile or so away.

Here Chinatown and the Bowery meet, and the Bowery used to be called that, because it was like a bower, and lovers used to walk there. Now it is a street of the poor, a street of cheap hotels, where men can lodge for twenty or thirty cents a night. In all the larger cities of the country they have such streets, and the migrants call them Skid Row. I believe the term originated up in the Northwest among the loggers who came to town with their pay envelopes and either put the skids under themselves or had them put under them by the liquor they drank and the company they kept.

It is the street of the poor, and there are pawnshops and second-hand-clothes stores. Here sailors, coal heavers, and dock workers without families come to live because they have not enough money to live elsewhere. Here are their cheap amusements, burlesque shows, movie houses, penny arcades, and their taverns. Here also the unemployed congregate because there is a thieves' market where anything can be sold, from a razor to a pair of pants. The very clothes on one's back can be sold and exchanged for overalls or dungarees. Here, too, men lie prone on sidewalks, sleeping off the liquor they have consumed, and here too are fights, and because of this, the street now has the name of a street of bums and panhandlers, drunks and petty thieves. But it is the street of the destitute, of the most abandoned. It is the street of missions, where for a confession of faith men are given a bed, and thus religion is dragged, too, in the mire, and becomes a word to gag over, an opiate of the people.

Here is Christ in his most degraded guise, spat upon, buffeted, mocked, derided. Here are temples of the Holy Ghost, men made to the image and likeness of God. Here are men, and while "Thou knowest, too, they are but dust, Thou knowest too, that Thou hast made them little less than the angels." . . .

Dorothy's description of her neighborhood with its different ethnic groups, its street vendors, and colorful street life continues on for several pages, which may be elided here, before resuming:

This is New York, one part of New York, with its seven million inhabitants. "Where seven million people live together in peace and democracy," one of the radio announcers used to say happily at the beginning and close of each day.

There is Harlem, of course, where close to a million of our population live in degradation and misery and unemployment. There is threat of class war and race war in Harlem. There are occasional battles between police and pickets in class war during strikes and lockouts. There are anti-Semitic meetings in Brooklyn and the Bronx and occasional fights at both.

But just the same, we all live in comparative peace and concord in New York City. If you count all the commuters who pour into the city every day, you can even say this is a city of nine million inhabitants. Canada has only eleven million people. There are truly too many people gathered together here in too little space.

And of all the congested streets in this most congested city in the world, Mott Street, Mulberry Street, and Bayard Street—these are the most congested. There are even more people here than in Harlem. And in Harlem people are so cramped for space that beds are rented in eight-hour shifts and several families share an apartment.

Mott Street, where we live, is half Chinese and half Italian. In our block between Canal and Hester there are a few factories, the offices of the Chinese Daily News, *a laundry, a lumber yard, a Chinese hall where a strange band practices, and a playground with a painted pond surrounded by trees and topped by a sunset painted on the brick wall on one side, and a jungle with all its animals on the other. These paintings and the fruits and the vegetables and fish on the pushcarts are the only splotch of color on this dark narrow street, full always with parked cars, children, boys playing games, men playing cards, and mothers sitting by baby carriages, winter and summer.*

Most of the time The Catholic Worker *office looks as drab as the street. The windows of the two stores, one the office, the other the coffee shop where we feed the bread line and the family of fifty who live in the house, are often streaked with steam and soot. The murals of the saints on the walls, painted by Ade Bethune some years ago, are much in need of freshening. The long tables and benches are a good part of the time filled with destitute men, on the one side and on the other the clerical and editorial work of the paper, and the receiving of visitors goes on from early morning until late at night. Upstairs there is another office, three- and four-room apartments for women, and in the rear house there are dormitories for men.*

Down here on Mott Street, half a block north of Canal Street and Chinatown, in the Italian section, in the most congested section, in the most congested city in the world, Peter Maurin, God's fellow-worker, prime mover in the decentralist movement in this country, has lived.

I had better tell everything I can remember of Peter Maurin and those early days on East Fifteenth Street, where I was living then. Who knows, he may be a saint, he may be a canonized saint some day, and we need a new kind of hagiography. This will be perhaps the basis of one of the lives of Peter Maurin that our children's children will read. I will try to remember all I can.

Peter is seventy years of age now [ed. note, 1947]. He was born in a small French community, two hundred miles from Barcelona, one of a family of twenty-three children. His own mother died after having given birth to five children, and his father married again, and there were eighteen more children. Amongst them now there are four teachers, three carpenters, some farmhands, and Peter has lost track of the rest. Some of his sisters are nuns and some of his brothers are religious.

Peter's name was Aristide Maurin then, but sometime or other in the course of his meanderings, he changed it to Peter.

Peter was baptized Pierre Joseph Orestide Maurin. In his village in France he was known as Pierre.[1] He apparently used the name "Aristide" in his early years in America. He may have changed his name to avoid French authorities, whom he feared may have been trailing him for draft resistance. Maurin's brother pointed out that for eighteen years, from 1907 to 1924, he did not contact his family, so eager was he to avoid attracting attention to himself or his family.[2] While writing this manuscript, Day may have forgotten that in a letter in 1933 she explained to a Fr. McSorley that Maurin had used the name Aristide until sometime after moving to Woodstock in 1926. At that time, after he had begun writing pamphlets and speaking in Union Square, he changed his name to Peter, an Americanization of his given name.[3]

He started wandering first as a cocoa salesman all over France. He did not visit any other part of Europe, though he certainly studied the history of Europe. When he came to Paris first he associated himself with a group of young men who flocked around Marc Sangnier, who headed a political movement called Le Sillon, the aim of which was, according to Peter, to introduce ethical principles into political life. The movement was afterward condemned, I do not know on what ground. Perhaps like Action Française, it was too nationalistic.

Probably it was the sight of the poverty of Paris slums, and the thought of his peasant background, and the reading of Prince Kropotkin, the Russian philosophical anarchist, that first led Peter to think of moving to Canada to settle on the land. He went there with a partner, who afterwards died, and Peter gave up the idea of homesteading.

Maurin was fifty-five years old when he met Dorothy Day. But it would be the following seventeen years he spent in her company that would give his life historic significance. Though Day dismisses two-thirds of the man's life with a few paragraphs, his first fifty-five years were hardly vacuous. Although he said little about his personal life, he did constantly remind listeners of his peasant roots. We know that this French peasant was born in the village of Oultet, department of Lozère, in the region of Languedoc. Dorothy Day in her biography quotes Maurin's own reflections on his childhood:

> *My mother's name was Marie Pages. She died in 1885. Of her five children, only I and Celestin, a brother who was eighteen months younger than I, and my sister Marie, two years younger than my brother, were left. My whole name was Aristide Pierre. Pierre was my grandfather and my godfather. He died at the age of ninety-four and he was never sick. He worked in the fields until he was eighty-five and after that he could not because of his eyes. So he stayed home and made baskets and recited his rosary. He liked to work. He knew it was good for him. . . .*
>
> *We did not eat the calves, we sold them. We ate salt pork every day. We raised no hops, so there was no beer. We raised no grapes, so no wine. We had very little meat. We had plenty of bread—there was a communal flour mill and bake oven. We had plenty of butter to season things with; we had no eggs. We had codfish from the Brittany fishermen. They went all the way to Newfoundland and Iceland to fish. We had vegetable soups, salads, and cheese. . . .*
>
> *My family owned eighty sheep and there was a herder for all the village who had an assistant in the summer. There were probably three thousand sheep in the flock, and they grazed on what was still communal land. The only garden near the home was for the chickens.*
>
> *It was very cold in winter. The fuel we used were branches from the trees. We used to cut the branches every three years. The leaves were for the sheep and the branches for the firewood. We cooked at an open fireplace.*
>
> *My father is dead, and my stepmother must be seventy-five now. Her name was Rosalie. She herself taught all the children to read and write. She was nineteen when she married my father. Last I heard, one brother was still farming there and dealing in cattle.*

The center of Oultet today.

I lived there in the southern part of France, a peasant, on the soil, until I was fourteen, and then I went away to school.

The brother Maurin mentioned passed the house on to his son, who currently lives there. Maurin was born on the second floor of this stone house. It is a substantial two-story house with a large barn connected to the back end. From the front porch is the view of Mount Lozère in one direction and in the other a vast, fertile valley, checkered with fields of wheat, grapes, and vegetables.[4] Maurin's nephew, a man of about seventy years, looks very much like the pictures of Peter Maurin at that age. Oultet is about twenty miles from the cathedral city of Mende, and sits on the side of a mountain. There are no more than twenty houses and families in the village, and half of them have the last name Maurin. In a village about two and a half kilometers down the mountain on the way to Mende is the town and church of St. Julien du Tournel. The churchyard

The Maurin home in Oultet, France. Window shows the second-floor room where Peter was born.

On Sundays Maurin and his family would walk down the mountain to the town of St. Julien du Tournel where they would go to mass.

includes a cemetery in which there are four plots belonging to the Maurin family. His grandfather's and grandmother's graves lie just to the right of the entrance to the church. Inside, a gray marble tablet hangs in the vestibule. It bears a list of those from the parish who died in the "Great War" and includes the name "J Bte (Baptiste) Maurin," Peter's brother, who died on May 25, 1917. Further inside the church to one side is the marble font where Maurin was probably baptized in 1877.

Emmanuel Le Roy Ladurie's classic, *The Peasants of Langue-doc*, may provide some insight into Maurin's early life, which is otherwise shrouded by his own reticence. One of the most revealing passages in terms of understanding Maurin is Ladurie's description of the communal nature of life in Languedoc. At least since the fifteenth century, "Friends, fathers, sons, joined themselves together in fraternities," Ladurie writes. "The common life was all-embracing: hearth, homestead, bread, wine, cooking pot, table, purse, debts, everything was shared. The money . . . was kept in a common coffer." Each "brother" had a key and a right to no more than five sous in pocket money." Ladurie points out that when one entered into a fraternity it was for life. It was an engagement of enormous import for each of the brothers, for their wives, and for their offspring.[5]

In his later life Maurin cited numerous sources to support his idea of the value of communal life. But these philosophers merely supported more basic personal instincts that had been nurtured from his earliest years. Arthur Sheehan, who knew Peter Maurin from the late 1930s until his death, also noted the influence of French communal society on Maurin. "Peter went back to the peaceful communes of France for his inspiration." Sheehan wrote that Maurin often wondered "why historians gave so much attention to the violent Paris story and so little to the peaceful life of the other."[6]

Maurin's earliest development was nurtured in the environment of the very type of church he advocated in his later years. As an adult he liked to quote the social encyclicals, particularly

Pope Leo XIII's *Rerum Novarum,* as evidence of Catholic responsibility for the oppressed. But even prior to the publication of that document in 1891, there were a large number of priests in his native France who advocated Christian alternatives to the economics of industrial capitalism. Writing in 1897, historian Pierre de Coberton noted that Christian socialism had made such progress in the previous decade among the French that a group had recently been formed which called for the formation of a Roman Catholic society of social economy.[7] Coberton also pointed out that on the occasion of the publication of *Rerum Novarum,* the workingmen of Paris made a pilgrimage to Rome to visit Leo XIII, whom they called the "workingman's pope." Accompanying the workers on this journey were members of a group called the Roman Catholic Youth.[8] At this time Peter Maurin was fourteen years old and living with the Christian Brothers. Given the environment in which he lived, word of this movement must have reached Maurin, and surely he was equally caught up in the enthusiasm for the new Catholic economic vision that was emerging in his country.

Maurin reached young adulthood at the time in France when Enlightenment sensibilities were clashing with Catholic tradition over the best way to ameliorate the social convolutions of the nineteenth century. There was rampant anticlericalism, yet there were also worker-priests organizing the downtrodden in cities and villages across the country. Catholics were fairly viewed as reactionaries, yet the Catholic economist Pierre Le Play founded the "Union of Social Peace" in order to give practical Christian expression to theories of social reform.

Two important social activists, Leon Harmel and Albert de Mun, helped plant the seeds of Catholic social thought in late nineteenth-century France. As a young man with a developing social conscience, Maurin could hardly have avoided the influence of these two men. De Mun had returned as a prisoner of war after the 1870 conflict with Prussia in time to take part in the suppression of the Paris Commune. Like many Catholics, he was horrified by the Communards' confiscation of the property of religious orders and the killing of many Catholic hostages, including the archbishop of Paris.[9] But de Mun was equally appalled by the bourgeoisie's utter lack of concern for the poor. Proclaiming that the labor problem was no longer a problem simply to be discussed but rather a crisis to be solved, he called for the formation of Catholic Workingman's clubs. "The men of the privileged classes have duties to be fulfilled with regard to their brothers, the workingmen," he declared.[10]

By 1873 there were seven workingman's clubs in Paris, and others in smaller cities of France. When the French General Assembly convened in 1875, the association had grown to 130 committees, 150 clubs, and 18,000 members. By 1900 there were 60,000 members, and the counter-revolutionary impulse that had led to the formation of the Catholic Workingman's clubs had been transformed into a detailed social program. It was a decidedly modern program, despite de Mun's own conservative inclinations, and he himself had become a leading advocate of social legislation in the chamber of deputies. Conservative clergy within the Church undermined de Mun's efforts to establish a new Catholic Party based on the defense of workers' rights, but after the publication of *Rerum Novarum* de Mun could cite the authority of a papal encyclical for what had appeared as his own personal and somewhat paradoxical compound of religious conservatism and social radicalism.[11]

Another important influence on Catholic social thought at the end of the nineteenth century was Leon Harmel, creator of the famous factory at Val-de-Bois. This factory attempted to realize what Victor Hugo had merely imagined in Jean Valjean's humane factory in *Les Misérables*. Harmel's factory functioned like a communal guild. Christian love served as its moral basis, and that spirit permeated a life of community. Each worker had a separate cottage and garden. Children were required to go to school until the age of twelve. Factory committees signed contracts with shoemakers, clothiers, coal companies, bakers, and butchers in order to ensure quality and fair prices for their consumers in the village. All workers, men and women, had accident compensation, life insurance, a bank account, and health insurance. Harmel's primary aim was the religious reformation of the industrial revolution. "Instead of attempting a vain and useless resistance," he declared, "let us go to the machine and baptize it!"[12]

Maurin was a teenager with the Christian Brothers when these new Catholic social thinkers emerged on the French social and intellectual scene, but years later, when proselytizing on the streets of New York, he would mention these two men in relation to the program he advocated. "Once upon a time there was a man by the name of Leon Harmel," Dorothy quoted his recollections in one of her articles. "He lived at the same time in France as Count Albert de Mun. The latter tried to reach the intellectuals and the former the workers. Leon Harmel came of artisan stock and he swore to bring his policy as employer into harmony with the teachings of the Gospels."[13] Quoting Leon Harmel in one of his "Easy Essays," Maurin wrote,

> The use of property
> to acquire more property
> is not the proper use
> of property.
>
> The right use of property
> is to enable the worker
> to do his work
> more effectively.[14]

And as an alternative to labor unions Maurin echoed de Mun's call for "Workingman's Associations that need to multiply and become more effective."[15]

Apart from the influence of these social philosophers, Maurin was equally affected by his life experience and the national character of his homeland. Peter Maurin was thoroughly French, and he celebrated his French roots. As Albert Feuillerat, a visiting lecturer at Yale, described his countrymen in 1925, "A

Frenchman unable to mingle with his fellows would cease to be a man. His best qualities would be atrophied. He would pine like a fish out of water. Even in a desert, his first idea would be to find someone with whom to live."[16] In the later, recorded years of Maurin's life, his personality certainly fit this description. Maurin engaged life on the streets. In writing a biography of Peter that began with a description of life on the street perhaps Day attempted to rescue the life of Peter from abstractions and restore a sense of his human context.

In 1909, at the age of thirty-two, Peter Maurin boarded the ocean liner *St. Louis* out of Cherbourg, bound for America. Part of the time on that trans-Atlantic voyage he must have reflected on the first half of his life. He probably recalled his trips to town with his father, a journey that began by walking down from the small mountaintop village of Oultet, where his house and about ten others overlooked the great valley and terraced gardens below, and to Mount Lozère above. At the bottom of the mountain, a few kilometers away, on a narrow winding dirt and stone road they would pass the church in the village of St. Julien du Tournel, where generations of Maurins lay in the front churchyard. Here they would arrive at the main road that took them along the side of the river Lot, which wound its way to the town of Mende. He probably recalled passing the thermal baths nearby at Bagnol-les-Bains where, ever since Roman times, visitors sought the healthy, restoring, and restful waters of the warm springs. Finally, after a journey by oxcart of about fifteen kilometers, he would arrive at Mende.[17] The town boasted a great fourteenth-century cathedral. It had been destroyed in 1562 by Huguenots and then restored through the generosity of Pope Urban V, whose statue today stands guard over the cathedral.

Maurin made the trip to Mende many times with his father, but the journey that probably remained etched in his memory was the one he took at the age of fourteen when his father left him at the recently built monastery of the Christian Brothers, which sat high atop Mount Mimmat, overlooking the town. The monastery covered no more than an acre of land. It included a two-story stone building of dormitories, refectory, and class-rooms. Alongside the main building, dug out of the mountain, were a kitchen and a barn, and directly in front stood a small chapel. As he walked around the grounds, where he spent the next five years, Maurin could look up to a grotto carved out of the mountain, which held the relics of St. Privat, a fourth-century martyr, or down below to the city of Mende, dominated by its proud cathedral.

One wonders what forces put Maurin on that ocean liner to the new world in the fall of 1909. We know that it was a bad year in the economic history of France, but that would have mattered little. From his childhood Maurin had lived in a subsistence soci-ety that put little emphasis on the accumulation of material wealth. However, facts from his early life also point to his frus-tration in realizing a life close to the spirit that drove him. His first frustration came with the Christian Brothers. Records reveal that after his initial training at the monastery of St. Privat in Mende he never stayed in one monastery more than a year, and never took his final vows.[18] Another disappointment came from the radical Catholic movements of Paris, about which he wrote critically many years later.

After leaving the Christian Brothers for good in 1902 he attached himself to the most influential and radical of these movements, Le Sillon ("The Furrow"). Led by Marc Sangnier, this movement of young Catholic intellectuals and activists had become an important voice in French social and political thought, as it would become an important influence on Mau-rin's early intellectual development. Le Sillon traced its roots to the publication in January 1894 of a literary monthly addressed "To the Younger Generation."[19] The editors characterized their era "as one in which the older generation had destroyed tradi-tional beliefs leaving behind only confusion." Urging a new renaissance, the magazine called on the younger generation to "put aside all sterile agitation and gather modest but resolute, humble but confident, like the grain which lies in the winter fur-row and ripens in silence the summer harvest which is to follow."[20] Shortly after reading this publication, Marc Sangnier, moved by its challenge, organized a series of student meetings to discuss social problems. At the first meeting, Sangnier declared, "We should become acquainted with one another, we should form a common soul and prepare ourselves together in a vigil of arms for a life dedicated to the people and to Christ." [21]

Born in 1873 in Paris into a wealthy Catholic family, Sangnier seemed to have been greatly influenced by his mother, whose single ambition, according to one biographer, was to make devout Christians of all her children.[22] He grew up surrounded by families much like his own, that is, wealthy and devoutly Catholic. At twenty-three Sangnier was "a bulky figure with a large head, blue eyes, and a drooping blond mustache." What was remarkable about this young man was his capacity for inspiring a kind of fanatic devotion in almost everyone with whom he came in contact. Those who remembered him recalled that part of his tremendous appeal was the complete commitment to his religious faith and the complete candor and directness with which he discussed it. Close friends called him "Marc the Apostle" or "Marc the Evangelist."[23] By his own admission not a great thinker, Sangnier claimed to have received his most important intellectual formation from two books: Blaise Pascal's *Pensées,* which he had always at his side, and Alphonse Gratry's *Les Sources.* The theme of the latter was that truth could be reached only through the use of all the faculties provided by God: "feeling, imagination, reason, love, and the light of revelation."[24] At Sangnier's urging, *Les Sources* became the bible of the Sillon movement. Aside from these books, he rarely read anything except current newspapers and periodicals.[25]

His lack of great ideas notwithstanding, Sangnier put together the most important Catholic social movement of France in the first part of the twentieth century. It envisioned nothing less than the conversion of the French republic to Christianity. The small study circles organized by Sangnier in the mid-1890s eventually grew into institutes where history, sociology, politics, and economics were discussed in the light of Christian values.

The view of Mende from the Monastery of St. Privat, where at the age of fourteen Maurin entered the novitiate of the Christian Brothers.

The first institute was located on rue Cochin, a little street between Boulevard Saint-Germain and the Seine, near Place Maubert. Members of the Sillon hoped to Christianize democracy through the formation of a social elite of young Catholics, enlightening the masses through popular institutes, public meetings, and organized political action. Leon Harmel was a great supporter of Sillon, and in 1903 he accompanied its members on a pilgrimage to Rome.

By 1905, circulation of the Sillon journal reached fifty thousand. Part of this popularity can be explained by a generation of young Catholics who, in protest against their parent's secularization of society, had undergone a new spiritual renaissance.[26] Maurin was also was caught up in this regeneration. He too wanted to proclaim the social message of the gospel in the streets. Apparently frustrated with teaching the children of the middle class, he left the Christian Brothers and soon after began meeting with the group that gathered on rue Cochin. He stayed with Sillon, selling their paper, attending institutes, and participating in rallies, for over three years. Describing the movement to Dorothy Day, he said simply that the Sillonists "were looking for an ideology. They were preoccupied about the idea of an elite in a democracy." Twenty-five years later Maurin revealed the influence this group's ideas of democracy continued to have on him.

> The elite in a democracy
> is imbued
> with what we call
> the right spirit.
> The democratic elite
> is the spearhead
> of a democratic society.
> The democratic elite
> is not moved by wealth
> or greed for power.

It is moved
by clear thinking.[27]

In 1906 Sangnier, in his efforts to further expand his political base, opened the movement to anyone who accepted the principles of Christianity, regardless of religious profession. It was soon thereafter that the movement, which had promised a new and dramatic element in the story of French democracy, came to an abrupt end. In August 1910 Pope Pius X condemned the Sillonist ideas of democracy and urged the resignation of its leaders and the submission of the movement to ecclesial control. Rather than submit, Sangnier and the Sillonists closed down the movement.

Maurin had already left the Sillon movement a few years before its dissolution. Most likely the new direction Sangnier had taken the movement did not coincide with his own developing ideas of how society ought to be redeemed. Commenting on this experience years later he simply said, "Sillon was full of enthusiasm and generosity, but lacked deep thought. It allowed itself to present democracy as the only political regime in conformity with Christianity. It was condemned for the preceding reason as well as imprudence in thought and action."[28]

Was it this disillusionment that led him to consider emigration? Was it, rather, as his brother suggests, a desire to avoid the draft?[29] Or was it, as Dorothy speculated, "the sight of the poverty of Paris slums, and the thought of his peasant background, and the reading of Prince Kropotkin," that led him to think of moving back to the land? Whatever the reason, in 1909 he came upon one of the many pamphlets circulating through Europe at the time advertising free land available for homesteading in Canada. For the last time in his life Maurin returned home to Oultet, where he gathered with his family to discuss his emigration.

2

Canada

ﾉ

I was always interested in the land and man's life on the land. That is why I went homesteading to Canada.

—Peter Maurin

Colonization companies had a long tradition in Canada. These entrepreneurs would buy tracts of land from the government at highly reduced rates. They would then publish brochures and set up offices from which they hoped to attract settlers. They would assist settlers in arranging transportation, getting supplies and whatever else they needed to get started on the land. Once there were a few people on the land working it, the remaining tracts could be sold at greater profit to the next wave of settlers.[1] Perhaps Maurin believed that this new land would provide the possibility for working out his own maturing vision of how society ought to be. So in the summer of 1909 Peter Maurin arrived in New York and immediately transferred to a train bound for Canada, where he would spend the next two years of his life.

His journey ended in the woods north of Prince Albert in Saskatchewan. Arthur Sheehan tells us that he arrived by train in Winnipeg with a Frenchman he had met at the port in Cherbourg.[2]

Maurin chose one of the most difficult places in North America to make a success of farming. He left no written record of life on the Saskatchewan plains, but others did, and these records provide some idea of the rugged life that Maurin faced. William de Gelder, a Dutchman from an upper-class family, arrived the same year and in the same place as Maurin, and kept a diary of his experiences. He described the vast treeless plains where he and his fellow immigrants found themselves as a "Prairie all flat land and not a single tree . . . for miles. In the distance you can see the mountains," he wrote, "[which are] about 40 miles from here. Because there are no trees wood is terribly expensive."[3] Since building materials were scarce, one can assume that there was not a great variety of architectural style; and everyone lived in similarly designed functional housing that could be built from the available materials. A house in Edenwold district described by Mrs. R. Miles probably would be typical. Mrs. Miles recalled living in a "big cellar about 3 or 4 feet deep," 12 feet wide by 16 feet long, which was dug out of the side of a hill. Over this large hole in the ground, settlers constructed a gabled roof made with poles. They then stacked hay about a foot thick on top of the pole framework, and on top of the hay, squares of sod completed the construction of the house on the treeless plain. They filled in gaps with a mixture of yellow clay and straw. The interior floor was six inches thick and comprised the same mixture of clay and straw and water, which the settlers patted down tight to the ground. The ceilings they plastered with mud and then white washed.[4]

Nothing is written about what Maurin raised on his homestead, but the staple was wheat. Pioneers also raised cattle on the prairie. However, as William de Gelder noted in his diary, "In order to buy or rent a farm you need[ed] a lot of capital. Everything is expensive here," he commented. "A work horse costs $300 a cow $40 and a chicken [costs] a dollar. The situation is entirely different from the one I read about in Holland," de Gelder complained.[5] Maurin probably thought the same. He did not arrive with a large amount of money so he could not engage in livestock or large-scale farming of wheat. Given his lack of

capital and his own background, he was probably more interested in subsistence farming, but even this was difficult in the
terrible weather that he experienced the two years there. Farming the land was not easy for Europeans accustomed to less
severe climates. As one historian has pointed out, "settlers from
more temperate areas had difficulties" adapting traditional
farming methods to the new environment.[6] Furthermore, statistics record that the two winters Maurin homesteaded in Canada
were uncommonly severe, even for Western Canada. Reports for
the twenty-year period from 1910 to 1929 reveal that the 7.9-
inch total rainfall for the year 1910 was the lowest in twenty
years.[7] Gelder's diary adds a human dimension to this statistic.
"This year (1910) has been very bad," he wrote. "If we get some
rain yet we can hope for 5 bushels an acre (in good times they
expect 20 bushels per acre) and that will just cover costs." He
added that the summer was "unbelievably hot, even in the early
morning. . . . The temperature reaches 110 degrees. Several days
ago it was 115 in the shade. (In the shade of the house that is,
there are no trees.) Everyone," he wrote, "is bothered by blazing
sun and blisters on the hands." Another "problem," he added,
"is the mosquitoes and other insects." Commenting on the long
hours of work he wrote, "Up in the morning at 4:30 or 5:00 we
work right through until 9:30 or 10:00 in the evening."[8]

And the winters were worse. As the Dutchman describes,
"It's been very cold the last couple of days 40 to 50 below. One
day it was 60 below in the morning and 52 below at noon. There
was a violent snowstorm which caused us to lose half a day [of
work on the railroad bed] and we continually had to watch each
other's noses and cheeks to warn of the possibility of frostbite."
Sometimes it was so cold, he wrote, "Half of a person's face was
snow white. Then you have to wash it vigorously with snow." His
feet were never warm, he continued, although he wore "three
pair of warm winter socks, a pair of sheepskin lined moccasins,
and over all that, elk skin moccasins."[9]

Peter Maurin, who was accustomed to the more moderate

temperatures of France, must also have been shocked to learn that the earth could reach such extremes of hot and cold. Furthermore, one must wonder how Maurin, whose meager funds did not allow him the luxury of extra clothing, could have survived the unbearable extremes of the weather.

Faced with the failure of their own crops and the possibility of starvation, many homesteaders hired themselves out to large farms and to wheat-threshing gangs. Arthur Sheehan mentions that Peter Maurin faced this reality, as did de Gelder, who described the experience in his diary. "You begin threshing at 4:00 a.m.," he wrote, "and finish at 9:00 in the evening." "At night," de Gelder recorded, "we sleep in a wooden shack about ¾ the size of a bath house lined with eight bunks each capable of sleeping two men."[10] "We thresh 1200 bushels a day," he recorded, and "the thresher gets eight cents a bushel. For this, the worker received $2.25 a day."[11]

The mathematics in this diary are not hard to figure out. Certainly de Gelder, a banker's son, was bothered by it, and surely resting in his two-man bunk after a long day of work, Maurin must also have contemplated his first recorded personal experience with capitalist exploitation. The owner of the thresher was receiving almost $100 a day, and the sixteen workers together shared a little more than a third of that.

Arthur Sheehan tells us that Maurin left his homestead after his partner died in a hunting accident.[12] This was probably only part of the reason. Had things been going well this setback would not have caused him to abandon the land. More likely the hard work, the isolation, the severe weather, and the failed crops, which produced little reward for the pain endured, had more to do with his leaving the land than a hunting accident. Also, this extremely lonely life did not fulfill the life of community for which Maurin yearned. Arriving without common heritage or common language and scattered on a vast unpopulated land, the European immigrants became terribly isolated. As de Gelder commented, "It's strange, but if the truth be told I don't know the people a hair better than when I first came here."[13] The experience must have left Maurin disillusioned. After living a number of years in Paris, witnessing what he believed to be the collapse of the bourgeois era, the opportunity to return to the land, to build an alternative life of community, was probably the most powerful of the forces pulling him from his home. But the harsh reality of the pioneer life on the plains of Canada destroyed this dream.

Like many who did not succeed on the Canadian frontier, he sought other employment: first as a thresher, then later with the Canadian Pacific railroad, which was plowing its way across the vast Canadian frontier at this time. For the inexperienced such as Maurin, railroad work was digging and picking—either clearing the path for the rails or digging irrigation ditches along the way. In 1912 F. A. Talbot wrote, "If one wishes to see the rough life of the wilderness at its best one must visit, live, and move in a railway camp. It is a strange albeit fascinating colony. There is an atmosphere of devil may care on every hand such as is met with in no other phase of human existence." Talbot described the "grader" as "a desperately hard worker who revels in the open air, enjoys toiling far beyond the limits of civilization, and who makes money plentifully. The camp has a cosmopolitan character," Talbot continued. "Every type of nationality will be met there. A little colony may represent as many as ten, fifteen, or twenty different tongues."[14]

Human kindness tempered the harsh railroad life, Talbot pointed out, as "various institutions such as the Young Men's Christian Association and the Salvation Army Mission have done yeoman service in improving the social conditions of the camp. Their magazines and books are circulated to gratify the desires of those who wish to read," he noted, and "a vigorous education campaign is maintained among the illiterate, while the foreign element is taught English."[15] Maurin's first lessons in English probably came from the YMCA or Salvation Army volunteers who visited the railroad camps.

A typical worker described by a visitor to the railroad project provides an idea of the life that Maurin may have been living at this time or how he himself may have appeared to an outsider. The home of this worker was "a small wooden shack barely eight feet square and was noisome to an extreme degree," the visitor observed, and he explained that the worker's "entire wardrobe consisted of a pair of tattered nether garments and a discolored mud stained flannel vest while his feet, from which socks were absent, were encased in heavy boots." He also noted that the railroad worker was "up with the sun" and by 4:00 a.m. he was "slaving away as if for dear life."

> His shovel swung regularly to and fro until the wheelbarrow was loaded. Then there was a short run up a narrow plank, a dexterous tilt, and the vehicle was discharged. Then he returned to the site and the process was repeated. He made no pause for meals but hurriedly swallowed some of the pork and beans an ample supply of which he carried in a tin pail. They were devoured while cold because they would have taken more precious time to eat had they been hot! He kept himself glued to his task until the shades of evening had fallen and the gathering mantle of night prevented him from seeing more than a yard before him.[16]

Working on the railroad provided a ready source of cash in an area where such opportunities were few. The men labored nine hours per day for twenty cents an hour, $1.80 a day or $10.80 for a six-day week. Five dollars was taken out for room and board, but the remaining $5.80 per week could be put away. In this way many young men saved their homesteads in the sparse early years of settlement. Maurin, however, must have put away his money in order to leave the dream that for him had become a nightmare. It was probably while working on the railroad that Peter Maurin met the Doukabors, described in Arthur Sheehan's biography.[17]

The Doukabors, or "Spirit Wrestlers," settled in Saskatchewan in 1899. By the time of Peter Maurin's arrival in

Peter Maurin, living in Chicago in 1917, about thirty years old.

1909, Norman Fergus Black, a contemporary observer of the Canadian frontier, wrote, "These peculiar people have been the object of so much public interest, sympathy, distrust and anxiety that the reader will probably welcome a discussion of their characteristics."[18] The Doukabors, Black continued, "are a sect who call themselves 'The Christian Community of the Universal Brotherhood.' The sect is of obscure origin," he noted. "It first attracted widespread attention of the authorities in the 18th century in certain Russian settlements north of the Black Sea." For political and religious reasons, the Russian authorities broke up communities in the Crimean peninsula and their members scattered through the Caucasus between 1841 and 1844. By the end of the nineteenth century this group, under the leadership of Peter Verigen, had created a Christian communitarian group based on internationalism, communism, and vegetarianism. A literal interpretation of the Gospels provided the basis for their beliefs. They also adhered to a strict policy of nonviolence. And because of their refusal to serve in the armed forces, the Russian government began another persecution of them. Their leader Verigen, along with many followers, was banished to Siberia.[19]

In a letter nominating the Doukabors for the Nobel Peace Prize, Tolstoy wrote, "A whole population, more than ten thousand persons, have come to the conviction that a Christian cannot be a murderer."[20] And for this, he observed, "they have suffered expulsion from their land, imprisonment and confiscation of their property."[21] Tolstoy began an appeal to collect funds to aid in their emigration from Russia. The Quakers of England made significant donations, as did Tolstoy himself, who donated the entire proceeds of his novel *Resurrection* to their fund.[22] Finally, in 1898, the czar gave the Doukabors permission to leave Russia. Texas, Hawaii, and Brazil were all considered as possible sites for a settlement, but someone had read an article by anarchist Peter Kropotkin that said Russian Mennonites on the Canadian prairies were thriving on good land in blocks that enabled them to live together. The Canadian government, pleased to welcome such hardworking, experienced farmers, promised asylum, exemption from military service, and set aside large tracts of land around what is now Kamsac and Yorkton.[23]

On January 24, 1899, the first group of Doukabors sailed into Halifax harbor, singing a prayer. They moved onto their land and built 57 villages of about 130 people each.[24] Without their leader, however, the community soon fragmented. One division was between those who abandoned their clothes as a symbol of their disinterest in material things and others who felt that such a demonstration in sub-zero temperatures was not a very good idea.

After his Canadian experience, Maurin finally found his way into the United States, where he would travel and work for another fourteen years, thus turning onto a path that would lead to cofounding the Catholic Worker. What influence did these two frustrating years on the Canadian frontier have on Maurin? His lonely existence in Canada must have convinced him more than ever that people were meant to live in community. Desperate for funds, he was forced to work as a thresher and as a railroad man and here for the first time, he came directly into contact with the harsh exploitation of industrial capitalism. His very concept of time must have changed in this period, as he learned to move to the mechanical demands of the clock rather than the organic rhythms of nature. He may have empathized with, and even been encouraged by, the communal life of the Doukabors, though their eccentricities and eventual fragmentation must have convinced him that to maintain cohesiveness a community must be drawn together by a substantive philosophy and belief system, such as Catholicism provided.

Many conquered the challenge of the rugged, lonely life of the Canadian prairie. They worked the threshers in the fall and the railroads in the winter; they saved their hard-earned money and realized the dream of owning and developing a homestead. For most in the Canadian frontier it was a hard, solitary existence, but the farm life of the rugged individual was not what Peter Maurin sought. So with money in his pocket he left Canada and searched elsewhere to realize his aspirations.

3

A Fateful Meeting

༄

When the organizers try to organize the unorganized
they do not organize themselves.
If everybody organized himself,
everybody would be organized.

—Peter Maurin

Penniless and once again landless, Maurin took to the rails, crossed the border into the United States, and for the next thirteen years worked as a laborer. Sometimes he achieved the comfort of the middle class; sometimes he lived in abject poverty, working in a coal mine and using an unused coke oven for a bedroom. Maurin talked little of these years.

In the Marquette archives there are a few scribbled notes taken by someone who lived at the Catholic Worker in the late thirties and interviewed Maurin about these lost years.[1] But little more exists. A *Commonweal* article written by Joseph Breig in 1938 contains the best account of this period of Maurin's life.[2] Breig wrote the article at the suggestion of Bishop Edward Carroll, who became impressed with Maurin's ideas and believed that someone ought to document his life for posterity. The reporter sought Maurin out and, sensing his reluctance to talk about his personal life, took great pains to gain his confidence. For his part, Maurin took a liking to the young man, and they became good friends very quickly. "Perhaps the fact that I had worked in a steel mill appealed to him," Breig surmised. Finally one evening, after suggesting that they get away and relax over a few beers, Maurin opened up to Breig and provided details of his itinerant life in America.[3] He described his first job in the United States in Ogdensburg, New York, tearing down concrete forms. He continued to reminisce, and over the next few hours he described the life of a penniless vagabond who worked for little more than sustenance and sometimes suffered imprisonment for the crime of being poor.

In his article Breig explains that Maurin worked his way through Washington, D.C., Maryland, the coal mines of Pennsylvania and the factories of Illinois, Missouri, and Ohio before arriving in Chicago. There, during the war years, he became moderately prosperous working as a French tutor and translator. But even this article, which carefully chronicles these years, contains little of interest to a biographer. It provides details of time and place, but little of reaction, reflection, or recorded memories of the events. Only once does Maurin provide some insight into his feelings or thoughts at the time. "I wanted a drink of water," he told Breig, "I knocked on a door. The woman tried to open it, but it was stuck with the frost. I started pushing to help her. The neighbors thought I was trying to break in. So to please the neighbors, the chief of police put me in jail. Two days later—to please the neighbors—he let me go." He often told of times he had been arrested during these years of his life. Possibly he repeated these stories because the horror of jail etched itself into his memory, but more likely he told these stories to make a point that being poor in this country of material promise and progress was in fact a crime.

Dorothy Day read Breig's article. Even though she admitted that it revealed more about Peter's "lost years" than anyone had known, the article troubled her. She did not like the title, "Apostle on the Bum," and she was perplexed—maybe even a trifle jealous—that Peter had decided to open up and "tell all" to a stranger, "a Hearst reporter." In his own defense, Peter shrugged and replied, "Joe Breig gave me a couple of beers."[4]

In her biography, she commented on Maurin's reticence regarding his own life. "It was hard to get Peter to talk about himself," she wrote. "He dealt 'with ideas, not personalities,' he used to point out impatiently." The person who knew him best, with whom he probably felt most comfortable, and with whom he might have shared his story, were he so inclined, was Dorothy Day, but the following is all she writes of those years.

He started to wander through Canada working with lumber camps and finally came down through New York State into the United States as one of a lumber gang. From the East he wandered to the Middle West.

He worked on railroads there, and on occasion he was thrown into jail. He told of one incident when he had been working somewhere down in Illinois and the job finished, set forth for Chicago where he was to be paid. The old biblical idea of not letting the sun set either on wrath or an unpaid workman is not in practice in our industrial system. The gandy dancers had to ride a freight, which was illegal, in order to get back to the city to get paid. On the way Maurin was arrested for vagrancy and trespassing on train property. Yes, Peter was well acquainted with poverty and injustice, rudeness and abuse.

He worked on farms, in brickyards, in steel mills, at every kind of unskilled labor, from Chicago to New York. At one time he settled in Chicago for a time and gave French lessons, using the methods as far as I can make out of the Berlitz School, and he was pretty successful at it. He read constantly, he worked, he taught. Always he was the teacher. He wrote out his ideas in neat, lettered script, duplicated them, and distributed them himself on street corners, an undignified apostolate.

According to his biographer, Arthur Sheehan, who also knew Maurin well, he settled in Chicago in 1914, where he worked as a janitor, as a dry goods store clerk, and from 1917 through 1925 taught French as a private tutor. But little else is reported, recorded, or revealed by Maurin. Even the city directories and census for those years do not reveal any secrets. Without documents, letters, or other confidences, the biographer is left frustrated. So much that would have contributed to his ideas happened in those undocumented years. In 1914 World War I broke out: his homeland was invaded, and one of his brothers was killed. One reason he left France was to avoid the draft; was his nonviolence now confirmed? Did he find solidarity with that small minority who did not rally to the call to arms? How did he feel about being in that very German American city of Chicago? He witnessed the great steel strike of 1919. Did he talk with the workers at any of the Chicago mills? Was he a worker at one of the mills? Did he work with organizers of the Chicago Federation of Labor? Did he know Mother Jones? Did he watch police break the heads of strikers with their billy clubs? Is this why he later wrote, "Strikes don't strike me"? During the Red Scare did he tremble in his small apartment wondering if he would be the next foreigner expelled? He spoke from time to time about the International Workers of the World (IWW). Did he join? Did he sit and share a bowl of Wobbly stew? Did he become a victim of the new nativism? There are no documents. The only source for these years was Maurin, and he refused to speak.

Once when pressed by Dorothy Day on these years he made the somewhat cryptic, somewhat provocative, comment, "I have not lived as a good Catholic all my life." Did Day know of some outrageous past in the life of Maurin? Did she keep it to herself (as she did the secrets of her own youth) so as not to diminish the significance of his ideas? If she did, she too took those secrets to her grave, and those years will remain the lost years of Peter Maurin's life.

Finally in 1927, at the age of fifty, we pick up his story again. Much we will never know, but one thing is certain: during these "lost years" he must have read voraciously on Catholic social thought, especially the rich ideas coming out of France in the twenties. Did he find a French bookshop in Chicago? Did he spend what little money he earned on reading the latest from Emmanuel Mounier and his new personalist journal, *Esprit?* None of this can be documented with certainty, but it is clear that by the mid-1920s, as a result of a lifetime of reading, working in various levels of the economy, and reflecting on the meaning of those experiences, Maurin went through a great intellectual and spiritual transformation.

In the mid-twenties one of his wealthy French students invited him to New York, where she promised to recommend him to others in her circle. He had settled into living a rather comfortable life as a translator and tutor in Woodstock, New York, when suddenly he abandoned this life and began working on a farm near Mt. Trempor that had been converted into a Catholic boy's camp. He spent his free time reading, writing out his thoughts, and traveling to New York City, where he began his one-man revolution to transform society.

The spiritual conversion is difficult to explain, but the intellectual roots of Maurin's synthesis can be documented. During this period Maurin began to write out his ideas in blank-verse form. When people were too busy to listen to him he would stuff these pieces of paper into their pockets for consideration when they had more time. Later these versed ideas were published in the *Catholic Worker* newspaper and as a collection entitled *Green Revolution.*

Many of his essays began with the words, "According to R. H. Tawny . . . ," or "Kropotkin says," or "Emmanuel Mounier wrote a book called. . . ." Another essay began, "If you want to know . . . ," and went on to reveal a bibliography ranging from Alexis Carrel's book on industrialism to Jacques Maritain's *Freedom in the Modern World.* This substantial bibliography blended with his own personal experiences: teaching with the Christian Brothers, attempting to Christianize the French republic with the Sillon, his first-hand witness of the injustices of industrial capitalism on the streets of the United States, and finally his certain disillusion with the bourgeois promise of comfort and harmony. All these experiences brought Maurin to conclusions he had spent a lifetime pursuing. He finally had a clear idea of the state of things and felt compelled to proselytize those theories.

In his verses he quoted medieval scholars and reveled in the lives of the saints and the Irish monks. For this he has been accused of idealizing the Middle Ages, but Maurin looked to the Middle Ages not as an idyllic past but rather as a model for creating a new society that could blend the material with the spiritual. As another biographer has written, he saw in the Church an institution with the resources both past and present "to carry on the struggle for eternity against the forces of modernity."[5]

Maurin proposed a reevaluation of the medieval synthesis that advocated the use of reason to arrive at an idea of eternity. Once validated through reason, this eternal vision would remind people of their common destiny, and this, in turn, would lead to concern for what Thomas Aquinas described as the "common good." Modernity had restricted human reason to material time and had negated the possibility of the infinite. Society had forsaken the common good in favor of individual progress. The result was an age of fragmentation and alienation.

Maurin incorporated the ideas of modern thinkers who supported his conclusions. He saw within the Church a positive expression of human solidarity in a rapidly fragmenting world. Among the writers who gave substance to Maurin's ideas were the Russian anarchist Peter Kropotkin, the French novelist Léon Bloy, and the personalist philosopher Emmanuel Mounier.

Kropotkin, born in 1842 to Russian nobility, abandoned his birthright at an early age and joined the Russian underground. Although he identified with the intellectual left, he did not follow the drift toward Marxism. He rejected the inevitability of class conflict, and in *Fields Factories and Workshops* (a book that Maurin paraphrased and printed out completely in Easy Essay form) he declared that class division did not represent the natural state of humanity. Kropotkin advocated a working place where scholars and workers might once again join together in the enterprise of human creation. From Kropotkin, Maurin borrowed one of his most popular catch phrases: "Scholars should become Workers so that Workers can become Scholars."

Kropotkin reinforced Maurin's apostolate to the working class. From his fellow Frenchman Léon Bloy, he borrowed the idea of the virtue of voluntary poverty. Bloy, an artist turned writer, spent most of his time in the decades around the turn of the last century in Paris, where he lived in the artist district of Montmartre under the shadow of the great basilica of the Sacred Heart. Bloy reveled in the power of the saints. "Saint Francis was not a poor man," he wrote; "he was in need of nothing since he possessed his God and lived through the ecstasy outside the world of senses." Bloy espoused the idea of voluntary poverty. It was not a new idea; in fact it was at least as old as the origin of monastic orders. But placed in the context of twentieth-century materialism, it was a sublime and yet solidifying protest. Maurin captured this theme in one of his essays when he noted, "while destitution isolated [people], poverty, as exemplified by the saints, monks [and nuns] of past ages, bound them together."

It is not hard to imagine Maurin, the young Sillonist, hearing of Bloy and wandering up to the Montmartre district to listen to the man, or sitting at a meeting of the Sillon discussing Kropotkin. It is easy to imagine these ideas planted in the young man's mind and then being fertilized and nurtured by his American experience. He experienced the injustices of capitalism; he experienced the isolation of a competitive society. He had sought comfort in the bourgeois promise, but found it wanting. And so at the age of forty-eight he had come to some important conclusions. He had concluded that the bourgeois dream that redemption comes through material progress was wrong, that humanity reduced to material progress was no longer human. His vocation would be to awaken people to that reality.[6]

Although Maurin's ideas reflect the influence of a variety of thinkers, those that best captured his synthesis were the French personalists, Emmanuel Mounier in particular. In fact, Maurin, who arranged for the translation of Mounier's *Personalist Manifesto*, is justly credited with introducing the personalist intellectual tradition into the United States.

Personalism was an expression of disdain for political economic structures as they were evolving in the early twentieth century. Specifically, it defined itself as a protest against all philosophies of materialism, including fascism, communism, and bourgeois capitalism. Personalists did not advocate supremacy of the spiritual over the material; rather, they sought to bring these two dimensions of human personality into greater harmony. They admitted that great material progress had been made in the nineteenth and early twentieth centuries, but it was at a spiritual cost that destroyed social harmony, setting poor against rich, worker against capitalist, and nation against nation.

The guiding social principle of the French personalists corresponded with the newly emerging Catholic image of the Mystical Body of Christ, a theory elaborated by the German theologian Karl Adam and which became recognized as a Church doctrine in 1943. The doctrine reminded Catholics that, as in a body, if one part suffers, all parts suffer. It was a call to a new human solidarity, a call to all Christians to an aroused and revitalized social conscience.[7]

In Europe, these ideas remained largely relegated to the universities and intellectual salons. In the United States, through the work of Peter Maurin, personalism took to the streets, and its influence filtered into various arenas of thought. Although seen as unrealistic by many, Peter Maurin's program seemed to him to be very practical. Personalism did not call for a mass political movement, but rather for individual action. Maurin began his one-man revolution talking wherever he could: from a Rotarian meeting in upstate New York, to a workers' rally in Union Square.

An important source for Maurin's practical personalism was the history of the Catholic Church itself. There was a time in the history of the Church, Maurin wrote, when it organized social welfare for the community. For the poor there were daily meals; for the homeless there were houses of hospitality. Given the current economic crisis, it was time, Maurin believed, to resurrect these social models. The Church needed to be reminded, Maurin said, of its historic role in issues of social justice. It was time for scholars to rediscover the history of the Church so that its social message could become the "dynamite" it was meant to be. He lamented the fact that the Catholic Church had been swept up in the rush for material prosperity, and in so doing had lost touch with its commitment to social justice. The apparent paralysis of the Church in confronting modern social inequities frustrated Maurin and convinced him that the laity would have to lead the redirection of the Church toward social issues.[8] It was time, he concluded, to "turn parish domes into parish homes."[9]

From 1927 until 1933 Maurin's message was rarely heard by more than the few unemployed workers who listened for entertainment in Union Square or by the random professor or economist whom he happened to buttonhole. But his meeting with Dorothy Day in 1932 changed all that.

Day, a writer and former socialist turned Catholic, took Maurin's message of Catholic social thought, added her own concerns for the emerging class struggle, and published *The Catholic Worker*. Within a year there was a circulation of fifty thousand, and Catholic Worker study groups or houses of hospitality flourished in every major city in the country. What attracted thousands of people to the Catholic Worker was not Maurin's sophisticated social analysis, nor the prospect of great political success, but rather his attempt to define a philosophy that went beyond the modern materialist synthesis. It called for an end to destructive competition and for a new economic community based on humanity's shared spirituality.

Dorothy Day, in her biography of Maurin, explains the impact this philosophy had on her. When she converted to Catholicism, she had no notion of the social message intrinsic to Maurin's theology. As a result, her conversion left her social conscience dormant. Maurin's synthesis created for Day a happy merging of apparently divergent interests. In her biography of Maurin she explains the intellectual and spiritual debt she owed him.

Dorothy Day's first meeting with Peter Maurin came in December of 1932. She had just returned from reporting on a "Hunger March" of the unemployed, which had taken place the week before in Washington, D.C. The trip made her realize how far her new faith had carried her from issues that had been central to her life. Communists, many of them her friends of years past, had organized the march. Now, for religious reasons, she now could not join her former allies, but only write about them. While in the capital she had visited the newly constructed shrine of the Immaculate Conception, and prayed there for a more meaningful way to integrate her love for the Church and her concern for social justice.

Upon her return Peter Maurin was waiting for her. He had been to the offices of *Commonweal* magazine, where he had waited all day to speak with the editor, George Schuster. He wanted Schuster to turn his Catholic magazine into a forum for his ideas on Catholic social thought. After listening to him, Schuster suggested he present his idea to Dorothy Day, the young journalist who sometimes wrote articles on social issues for *Commonweal*. Maurin left the *Commonweal* offices without her address but somehow found her. He returned every day to her apartment, convinced that she could be the person who would help give his ideas a greater hearing. But first she would need a good Catholic education, one grounded in Catholic social thought. This he would provide. Day's account begins:

I was settled in my home, cooking, ironing, sewing. Women are always putting their roots in. I had learned to live in slum tenements. I had learned from my life in the radical movement the freedom of poverty. There was the richness of poverty too, there on Fifteenth Street, with its backyards, and little fig trees and peach trees, petunias and widows' tears and privet hedges that smelled acrid sweet in their blossoming time.

It was my home; the church was around the corner. It was the time of the Great Depression, the depths of it by 1933, and my brother and sister-in-law were living with me. My little daughter was six years old, just starting to go to school. I was doing research work on war and peace, and my work took me to the library every day from nine till three. At home it was fun to sew for the new baby my sister-in-law was expecting. We were comfortable and settled and happy in spite of the Depression, with the happiness of unthinking women who accept things as they are, who are happy with children and a warm house and supper cooking on the stove.

For seven years I had been a Catholic. My brother and sister-in-law at that time were Communists. My friends were Communists or fellow travelers, and I didn't know any Catholics except the parish priest to whom I never spoke outside of the confessional. I read Karl Adam, St. John of the Cross, St. Teresa of Avila, St. Augustine and the Imitation of Christ. I knew of the social teachings of the Church, but I felt that eternal life was more important than this present life, and besides, I was enjoying the present life. I was a convert Catholic; I could no longer work with the Communist party as I had a few years before. The last job I had had with them was working for the Anti-Imperialist League, which was calling attention to American aggression in Nicaragua. But I knew no work I could do within the framework of the Church. I had done newspaper work, writing articles, doing research, covering labor conflicts, working long hours for small wages as a Catholic. It was solitary work.

And then Peter came to be my teacher, to disturb my content, to remind me that we are pilgrims, and that we have no right to dig our roots in.

For a long time Peter had been collecting those who would listen. For the past seven years he had worked at Mt. Trempor boys' camp, mostly winters as a caretaker as far as I could gather. It was hard to get Peter to talk about himself. He dealt with ideas, not "personalities," he used to point out impatiently.

Dorothy Day reading to her daughter, Tamar, in 1932,
around the time she first met Peter Maurin.

*Leading out from this subject of work, he could talk for hours on
a "philosophy of work," "the dignity of work," personalism, communitarianism, Benedictinism, prayer and work, Marxism and pro-
letarianism, on selling one's labor.*

*He could talk on all these things, give a lecture before a seminary
or college or convent or monastery on such subjects, but he would
never illustrate with the particular. That is why I think it is necessary to tell of the Peter behind these ideas. The incidents I tell of give
the ideas "points," as he would say himself. Peter, although a humble*

man, liked to add prestige to his points. He liked to quote authorities for his ideas, none of which he claimed were original with himself. He made a synthesis in the material order.

But to me, being a woman, the ideas were not dynamic unless they were illustrated with incident. And often Peter provided no incident.

There was no stopping Peter, he went on night and day. He slept until noonday mass and was filled with energy for the nights when the workers were free. But he would have, and often did, keep going until two and three in the morning if we did not call a halt.

It was not only that he was single-minded. I suppose he did not have what the world calls manners. He was oblivious to the little things. He was a French peasant, and if he was in a drawing room it was because he had something to say. Manners were not important, and he would walk first through the door, forget to take off his hat, not give up his seat to a woman unless he were told, nor say thank you when given anything. He was unconscious of the need for such courtesies. Or perhaps he did not have the habit of them. He was not self-conscious about his lack of manners either. To him, "a gentleman was one who did not live off the sweat of someone else's brow." He liked to talk of "the gentle personalist," and once when we were distributing literature during a strike, and were ridden down by the mounted police, Frank O'Donnell turned to the rest of us and said clearly with lifted brows, "Don't forget you are all gentle personalists."

We gathered people together as we went along together, Peter and I. He talked to me and to my sister-in-law every evening, because my brother was at that time working nights. He lectured me, he talked to me, and he read aloud to me. And often I found it wearisome, of course. You cannot live at that intellectual level all the time; your mind gets tired.

His conversation was not always made up of an outline of history. He also had a memorized series of essays such as those on Houses of Hospitality, Farming Communes, Caesarism and Personalism, etc. He brought not only the books he thought people should be using, but also when they would not read the books, a summary

*of them, a series of his own phrased writings, containing the essence
of the books. We have notebooks now with all of Eric Gill's works
synopsized and phrased.*

*Even this was too much for many of us, his chosen students, so
then he started his synthesis of "Cult, Culture, and Cultivation."
From the nearest stationer's shop he purchased his pad and paper,
and then in pencil neatly headed three sheets: the first "Cult," the
second "Culture," and the third "Cultivation." Then on each of these
sheets he would phrase some thoughts from authors to fit under these
headings. For instance, the first page would contain some quotations
from Bede Jarret on faith, the second from Eric Gill on art, and the
third from Kropotkin,* Fields Factories and Workshops. *If he found
listeners, he would read them these three pages and invite discussions. Or he would leave the pages for his pupil to read.*

*When Larry Heaney, who is now with a farm group in
Rhineland, Missouri, was living on the Easton [Catholic Worker]
Farm, Peter used to send him three pages a day through the mail to
tack on the bulletin board for all on the farm to read and ponder.
Peter would have liked a formal discussion to be going on in connection with his synthesis, for though he hated what he termed organization, he dearly wished that people would organize themselves to
study together.*

*He organized himself. He was always ready and available as a
teacher, but the rest did not naturally follow. People are looking for
organizers, and when they think that they have gotten past that
themselves, they become anarchists rather than self-organized, self-
disciplined communitarians.*

*That was one of Peter's great troubles, always. People took part
of his idea and made it their own and clung to it tenaciously. "Fire
the bosses," they would say triumphantly, and that meant that they
would accept no leadership whatever. This defiance gave them great
comfort in time of Depression, when there were no jobs anyway.*

Visitors would come in: Michael Gold from the Daily Worker,
*his brother George Granich, who organized the New York delegation
of the Hunger March which had gone to Washington that fall.
Tessa's sisters who were working, one in the labor movement and one*

tracing art, used to drop by. After we began publishing the Catholic Worker *our Communist friends left us. When religion was a private matter with us it was all right to come and pay a call. But when Peter and I became editors of a paper, we were enemies. After that first year many friends fell away.*

Peter was a teacher and undoubtedly it is proof of his genius that he left so much for people to find out for themselves by their own reasoning. He held a high ideal, and was not disillusioned when they only reached half way. At any rate, they had made a start. He leaped as it were from crag to crag of thought, expecting his listeners to think and fill in the gaps. Often it made them only disjointed in their own reasoning.

The books Peter brought us enriched us immeasurably. Besides Eric Gill, there was Jacques Maritain, Léon Bloy, and Charles Péguy of France, Don Luigi Sturzo of Italy, Romano Guardini of Germany, Nicholas Berdyaev of Russia. He opened our minds to great horizons, and he gave us a vision.

He never tired of teaching, and many were the meetings held in the store, which was the office of the Catholic Worker. *Night after night, those first years, the meetings went on, from eight to ten, often far later. We, who had been up since before seven, were often yawning and ready for bed.*

I remember one time leaning wearily over the kitchen table, listening to the voices beyond the door in the long store. Stanley Vishnewski, a young Lithuanian boy, and Mary Sheehan, who sold papers on the streets, were drinking coffee. "Gee," said Stanley, in an awestruck voice, "if he were teaching at Fordham now, how much money he would get for these hours of teaching he puts in."

"And why aren't we out there listening to him, if he's so great?" Mary said in her usual tart way. But we went right on drinking our coffee and I was longing for the meeting to be over to go to bed.

Maurin did not remain in New York City. From time to time he would wander back to where he had been living for seven previous years in a boys' camp. At the boys' camp Maurin did odd jobs in exchange for room and board and a few dollars that he spent on journeys to New York City. Day describes this life as she observed it:

> As far as I could gather, he lived with the horse in the barn. He mended roads, broke rock, cut ice, and stored it in the icehouse. He did the rough work that he could do on his own. He always worked on his own, both because he was independent of spirit, also because he could never bear to "boss a job." He called himself a communitarian, but first of all he was a personalist who wished to guide by example rather than by orders. He wished to be "what he wanted the other fellow to be," as he used to put it in one of his essays.
>
> We used to laugh about Peter's "points." He liked to see things come to a crisis because then he could make a point. He was trying to make the "encyclicals click," he would say, smiling delightedly, like a child at a neat phrase.
>
> When he got tired of his solitary and healthy life on the land, with his horse, his books, his soup, he would come to New York, where the priest for whom he worked had a big parish on the Upper West Side. This priest used to call Peter his "man Friday," and liked to tell of the conversations he had with Peter.
>
> When Peter lived in New York, he did not live in the rectory uptown, which was carpeted with soft rugs and had uniformed maids to answer the door. He lived on the Bowery in a flophouse, and the priest gave him a dollar a day to live on. This dollar was supposed to cover three meals as well as bed money.
>
> Often the priest was not there, and Peter went without. I had understood that this was an old arrangement between them; not that Peter was a pensioner, but that he gave his services in the country. And then the priest financed him for his stays in the city when he went about the city squares to be a lay apostle, to spread the social teachings of the Church, to reach the man in the street. Besides stopping into the sacristies of all the churches where he heard a sermon he particularly liked, besides haunting rectories and diocesan newspaper offices, Peter used to indoctrinate in Union Square. It was there as well as from George Schuster that he heard of me and came to indoctrinate me, to give me an education with a Catholic background.

But when I wrote a little note to the priest once saying that Peter had received nothing for the past thirty days and was behind in his thirty cents a day bed money, I received a curt little note, saying that the priest was not responsible for Peter's debts.

I have hesitated to mention this for fear the little worm of bitterness might be there on my part to muddy the tale. But I feel I must tell it, to illustrate the reality of Peter's poverty, which has had with it the rebuff, the insults even, that all the poor must suffer in times of destitution. He loved this man and had confidence in him. He was always quoting him as an authority on education and telling of the wonderful things he was undoubtedly going to do some day in the cause of education. But as soon as money entered the relationship, as soon as I brought up the suggestion that he might be responsible for Peter's living for a period, he shied away as though he had been touched on a most tender spot.

Money! It is indeed a most tender subject. "God or money," a new translation of the New Testament puts it, instead of "God or mammon." Money comes between people like a wall. I remember once calling up a well-known newspaperman and asking him to come see an old man who was dying in our hospice who had been Sunday editor of various newspapers, and who often spoke lovingly and admiringly of his friend. But when I telephoned, the journalist said hurriedly, "He is no relation of mine. I am not responsible for him." He had been afraid he might be asked to pay debts or bury him or share with him in some way his money.

After that little incident, Peter continued to sleep in his cheap hotel, thirty cents a night, and depended on any chance encounter to keep a roof over his head. Friends did not mind being "touched" for thirty cents. It was responsibility that they shunned. Being responsible for each other. "Am I my brother's keeper?"

I have no doubt but that Peter felt keenly such rebuffs and reproaches: "Why don't you get a job?"

> Why don't you work like all other men do?
> How can I work when there's no work to do?
> Alleluia, I'm a bum,

Alleluia bum again
Alleluia give us a hand out
To revive us again.

These are the words to an old song of the Industrial Workers of the World, and the word *bum* was often applied to Peter. Indeed there was an article in Commonweal called "Apostle on the Bum," which painted a very good picture of him. Only I objected to the word "bum."

Year after year, since 1933, Peter has spoken in seminaries and colleges and has been given modest offerings and has had his fare paid from place to place. Had he worn a dress suit, carried a suitcase, stayed at a good hotel, his offerings would have turned into fees, and the respect accorded him been greater.

I write these things, not with bitterness, I assure you, but to make the point that Peter often makes, that poverty should be respected, that we should see Christ in every man regardless of dress suit. Intelligence and sanctity are apparent to many, thank God, in spite of clothes. Peter's old suit, a cast-off of someone else, his little dollar suitcase full of books and pamphlets to lend weight to his points, his beaming, radiant, serene face, these all came to be loved in many a circle around the country.

And who were some of his friends when I met him? He used to go with ideas written out to meet people of importance. I know only the ones who received him and loved him, but he certainly must have visited many in the seven years he was coming from the camp up the Hudson to the city where he sought a place in the apostolate where he would not be alone.

There was Mr. Woodlock, editorial writer for the Wall Street Journal. He always received Peter with courtesy and interest, and they had many a conversation together. Mr. Woodlock is dead now, but I am sure he contributed to Peter's thought, as I know Peter contributed to his. Mr. Thomas Aquinas Woodlock they used to call him at the Wall Street Journal, and it was of the Thomistic idea of the common good that he and Peter used to speak.

Then there was John Moody of Moody Investor's Service. Mr. Moody and his family became warm friends of Peter and of the work

*of the Catholic Worker movement, which Peter founded. I haven't a
doubt but that Peter talked of money, of the morality of using money
to make money, of a philosophy of work, of the rich and the poor, of
state responsibility and personal responsibility and works of mercy,
in addition to the social teachings of the encyclicals. And I don't
doubt either but that he discussed ownership by the worker of the
means of production, and an ownership that brought responsibility
and not a share in the stock, which was a bribe, a sharing of profits, "a stock which got the worker all stuck!" Peter used to end triumphantly, his face beaming, thinking he had made an especially
clever play on words.*

John Moody wrote that Peter Maurin was always an inspiration. "My love for his forthrightness, his remarkable straight-
thinking mentality, with the noble self-denying life he led, grew
stronger all the time. He indeed . . . is the one who is truly living
the Christ-like life. And of course his talent for expressing himself on paper, so full of wisdom, logic, and true Catholic philosophy, has been a continual inspiration to me. . . ."[10] Moody, the
investment broker, was one of the many well-known and not so
well-known persons whom Maurin contacted on his personal pilgrimage. Whether in Union Square or Wall Street, Maurin relent-
lessly pursued his mission. Finally after seven years his persistence
was rewarded; he had found Dorothy Day, and she would become
the person who would provide the vehicle for his ideas.

*He stressed simple and fundamental truths, so simple they
seemed obvious, and so powerful that they contained the energy to
change people's lives, provided they are spread by people who really
believe in them. It is this faith that makes them dynamic.*

*Perhaps that is what makes Peter so important a person, this
tremendous faith he has, not only in God, but also in men. He was
an apostle to the world. It is this which set him apart from other
men, from other saints of the Church who went around preaching
penance, reminding men of their relationship with God and eternity.*

Tamar, Dorothy, and Peter, around 1935.

Peter thought not only in terms of eternity, but of this present life, where we are actors, where we are placed as though in a testing ground, to prove ourselves, to prepare ourselves for eternal life.

Peter so felt the tremendous importance of this life, that he made one feel the magnificent significance of our work, our daily lives, the material of God's universe and what we did with it, how we used it.

The dignity of the worker, the dignity of work, the goodness of God's goods, man as a co-creator, these were the things he believed in. He had faith in himself, in his own importance as a lay apostle, and that faith was sufficient for him to rise above any and all rebuffs from whatever source they came. He was confident he had a message. He always talked of the necessity of the long view, of the vision, in order to give ourselves the perspective we needed to see things in the light of eternity. That very long view made the work of the day, what we did here and now, so important that each thought, each decision, each step we took determined the future, not only for ourselves but for the world. "For the others."

Charles Péguy, to whose writings Peter introduced us, was always mindful of the "others." He used to say that when he appeared before God, God would say to him, "Where are the others?" So the problem was how to reach them, how to influence them. "By being what you wanted the other fellow to be," Peter said simply in one of his little essays. Peter was no empty cistern. He was not giving what he had not got. The divine life was in him. He was so conscious of that overwhelming fact that he was a child of God, an heir of heaven, that he made others feel it.

"By the feast of our baptism we are partakers of divine life," he would remind us. "Grace is like the blood of Christ in our veins. Our relationship with each other is closer than that of blood."

The Christ life was in us, yes, but not as it was in Peter. In one of the retreats Fr. John J. Hugo gave us some years after, he spoke on this mysterious subject of grace. "Many people say, 'It is enough to remain in the state of grace; just don't fall into mortal sin. That is enough. I don't steal, murder, commit adultery; I'm getting along all right. So I'll just enjoy life and heaven too. God put us here to be

*happy. So I'll get mine. Just as long as I stay in the state of grace."
That man, Fr. Hugo warned us, "is like an imbecile child. Can one
conceive of a mother being comforted over the fact of her imbecile
child by anyone saying to her, 'Anyway he has life.' She wants him
to grow. She wants him to grow in life. It is the same with us. To be
partakers of the divine life is not enough. We must grow in it."*

*All of us who have worked with Peter these past fifteen years [ed.
note, 1932-1947] feel that Peter is one of those who have grown in
divine life, while we have been but babes. Where has been our faith in
our own dignity as men, temples of the Holy Ghost, made to the
image and likeness of God, partakers of divine life, brothers of Christ?
We have not felt it in ourselves, let alone in our brothers, in the
Negro, the Mexican, the Filipino, the Japanese, the Chinese, the
Indian—any of another color, another culture than our own.*

*And certainly this failure to see Christ in the worker has brought
about the heresy of Communism, which overemphasizes, as all heresies do, one aspect of the truth.*

*One needs to feel his own dignity in order to see another man's.
Peter is an example of this; he did not hesitate to go anywhere or
speak to anyone. He never thought of clothes, letters of introduction,
and the background of money or family. "A man is a man for all of
that," he used to quote, and whereas many of us used to think he was
talking in platitudes, he uttered a terrible and profound truth.*

*"The truth needs to be restated once every twenty years," Ibsen
said. And Peter brought these commonplace truths home to us. And
that is why he made his impress on the world, on his fellow man, so
that we who worked with him, in many cities, on many farms, and
in many groups, found in him a wandering apostle, a lay apostle, a
leader, and have wondered perhaps if he is not one of the saints of
our day.*

*And that is the reason for writing this book. That is the reason
for publishing it, for circulating it. Maybe some of its ideas will have
the profound effect on us that Peter himself has had.*

4

The Catholic Worker Begins

ろ

The Catholic Worker believes
in creating a new society
within the shell of the old
with the philosophy of the new
which is not a new philosophy
but a very old philosophy,
a philosophy so old
that it looks like new.
　　　　　　　　—Peter Maurin

Although their initial meeting did not leave Dorothy Day with the fervor of a convert, she gradually came to see in the peculiar man's ideas a philosophy of social vision that not only was as radical as her own, but which was also Catholic. In her later book, *Loaves and Fishes*, she summarized his message:

We were to reach the people by practicing the works of mercy, which meant feeding the hungry, clothing the naked, visiting the prisoner, sheltering the harborless, and so on. We were to do this by being poor ourselves, giving every-thing we had; then others would give, too. Voluntary poverty and the works of mercy were the things he stressed above all. This was the core of his message. It had such

*appeal that it inspired us to action—action which certainly
kept us busy and got us into all kinds of trouble besides.*[1]

In her biography of Maurin she outlined his practical plan of
action, as she understood it:

*Peter Maurin's program of action, in the face of the crisis of the
day, a crisis that has continued these last fourteen years through a
great depression and a war, remains the same now as it did when we
first met back in 1933.*

1. *To reach the man in the street with the social teachings of the
   church.*
2. *To reach the masses through the practice of the corporal and
   spiritual works of mercy, at a personal sacrifice, which means
   voluntary poverty.*
3. *To build up a lay apostolate through round-table discussions
   for the clarification of thought.*
4. *To found Houses of Hospitality for the practice of the works
   of mercy.*
5. *To found farming communes for the cure of unemployment.
   To solve the problem of the machine, for the restoration of
   property and the combating of the servile state; for the building up of the family, the original community, the first unit of
   society.*

During that first winter, Maurin appropriated Dorothy's
apartment for use as the first "House of Hospitality," where an
unemployed worker might find a cup of coffee, some warm soup,
and possibly a place to lay his head. The house also served as a
forum for round-table discussions, where Peter could clarify his
ideas. Dorothy describes in the following section what had
become of her house in that first winter with Peter Maurin.

*There was a mad sculptor who used to come in whom I must
speak of because telling of him illustrates one aspect of Peter which*

is not only amusing but often irritating and causes complications in the work we do now in running houses of hospitality and farms.

Homer the sculptor also played the flute. He would drop in on an evening and while Peter talked, he would take out his flute and play. When Peter spoke to him especially, when he thought Tessa and I were not attentive enough, the flutist would answer with some unintelligible remark, which somehow satisfied Peter so that he went on. Once when a woman friend paid a call and was introduced to Homer, he acknowledged the introduction and said courteously, "Yes, I think I met you in Paris last year. You were sitting quite nude on a mantelpiece."

Of course he was mad. The poor woman, the respectable mother of three children, was overcome with confusion. The rest of us had known Homer long enough to know his harmlessness and to put up with such artist's vagaries. A sculptor probably saw people as nudes. But Peter paid no attention to such remarks. Either he did not hear them or perhaps he believed them, expecting anything of anybody, and perhaps assuming the new caller to be an artist's model. Anyway, nothing interrupted his flow of speech, his ideas that he was trying to clarify for the benefit of the group. In his naiveté he thought everyone was anxious to listen, anxious to learn, anxious to participate in the apostolate he was anxious to start. He could not conceive of anyone being indifferent to ideas, as desirous of entering into light conversation. If we started talking of children, clothes, gossip, he would relapse into silence, his speech would become a "yea, yea," and a "nay, nay."

Later he would wander off with Homer and his flute, and the two of them would spend the rest of the night on a bench in Union Square, Peter, with his monologue, and Homer, with a gentle and slightly mournful accompaniment. Who knows what souls they reached, the two of them, those nights of the winter of '32 and '33.

By mid-winter 1933 Dorothy Day knew what she was going to do. Peter's idea of a newspaper filled with ideas on Catholic social thought captured her imagination and she determined to have the first edition of such a paper ready for distribution on May 1, the international workingman's day. From the first edition the paper was Dorothy's, not Peter's. Maurin wanted a paper that would carry nothing but his essays, which interpreted the contemporary social economic crisis of the 1930s in the context of the great Catholic social thinkers. But Dorothy's paper included news of strikes, personal accounts of workers, and her own personal column along with Maurin's essays. Even the name of the paper, *The Catholic Worker*, was her decision. Maurin had preferred the name *Catholic Radical*. Reflecting on the difference in their perspectives, Dorothy later observed,

> *He was a Frenchman; I was an American. He was a man twenty years older than I and infinitely wiser. He was a man, I was a woman. We looked at things differently. He was a peasant; I was a city product. He knew the soil; I the city. When he spoke of workers, he spoke of the men who worked at agriculture, building, at tools and machines which were the extension of the hand of man. When I spoke of the workers, I thought of factories, the machine, and man the proletariat and slum dweller, and so often the unemployed. . . . It was amazing how little we understood each other at first.*[2]

When she finally completed the first edition, and paid for its publication with her rent money, she proudly presented the paper to Maurin, who glanced through it and said, "It's a paper for everybody." Then, after a pause, he commented, "Everybody's paper is nobody's paper."

Maurin left Dorothy, and for a while tried to found his own House of Hospitality in Harlem, but eventually returned to the movement that she was beginning with his inspiration in lower Manhattan. Although she mentions this incident in her autobiography, *The Long Loneliness*, she left it out of her manuscript on Peter Maurin.

For Maurin's biography she created a different version of the paper's origin:

> *"To reach the man in the street"—that was Peter's first step. "The workers of the world have been lost to the church," Pope Pius XI is reported to have said to Canon Cardijn, international head of the Young Christian Workers. It is here that the apostolate of the word comes in, newspapers, leaflets, and magazines. Peter suggested the publishing of a paper, to be called* The Catholic Radical, *or perhaps* The Catholic Agronomist, *but since I was to do the job of editing, I finally selected the title and called it* The Catholic Worker. *I have since then learned of the distinction Eric Gill and Chesterton and others of his school made between the titles "worker" and "workman," and can understand Peter's distaste for the word.*

Here Day quotes a letter from her son-in-law, a member of the Catholic Worker, on the meaning of the word "worker," still justifying her decision fifteen years after making it.

> *David Hennessy, who is a collector of Chesterton, Belloc, and Gill, writes me: "As for Gill's distinction of the words 'worker' and 'workman,' I don't know of any one full quotation in his writings, though he uses the term 'workman' and not 'worker.' It is Chesterton whom I always quote about those two words. In his book of essays,* As I Was Saying, *published just three days before his death—in essay XXVIII 'About the Worker' he refers to Eric Gill as England's first workman. Note how both those twin evils, Communism and capitalism, use the word 'worker' inhumanly—for Jim the horse is a good worker, but the workman will be found used by those of the faith, such as Leo XIII, Pius XI, Belloc, G. K. Chesterton, Eric Gill, and even Cobbett of the Church of England."*
>
> *As the journalist in this new partnership between Peter and me, I selected the name mostly because I considered there to be only two philosophies, that of the Marxists and that of the Catholics, and I wanted to use the name "worker" as common to each. Eric Gill himself in writing to us never criticized the name.*

Union Square readers of *The Catholic Worker.*

Having justified her decision for the name Day notes the movement's early success:

The Catholic Worker *has aroused opposition because of its title, but it has also become popular, and was adopted by groups in England and Australia who also published papers by that name and feel themselves to be part of what has come to be called the Catholic Worker movement. Peter is acknowledged to be the founder and head of the movement:* The Catholic Worker, *a monthly, has been distributed from the very first in public squares, sold on street corners, distributed in front of meeting halls. At times the circulation, which started at 2,500, went up to 150,000 at a time when labor was beginning to organize and there was a greater call for the paper for mass distribution.*

Now (thanks to Maurin) Day had a Catholic philosophy to support her radical inclinations. Her conscience reconciled, she returned with new enthusiasm to an old devotion. In the early thirties those fighting for social justice endorsed and supported industrial unionism. This crusade distressed Maurin. Influenced by an earlier generation of French Catholic social activists, Maurin condemned collective bargaining, which merely turned workers into capitalists. Maurin was looking for an alternative economic structure. "Strikes don't strike me," he told Day. Perhaps in addition to early French influences it was also the memory of the violence of the Steel Strike of 1919 that affected his opinion because in 1936 when the newly formed CIO introduced the sit-down strike in an apparent turnabout, he supported it. In one of his Easy Essays he wrote:

> Strike news
> doesn't strike me,
> but the sit-down strike
> is a different strike
> from the ordinary strike.
> In the sit-down strike
> you don't strike anybody
> either on the jaw
> or under the belt,
> you just sit down.
> The sit-down strike
> is essentially
> a peaceful strike. . . .
> It may be a means
> of bringing about
> desirable results.

Dorothy Day confessed Maurin's opposition to unions, and justified her own activist role.

At those times when such simple issues as the rights of workers to organize into unions of their own choosing were at stake, it was

*very necessary to get into industrial conflicts, in front of factories
and on picket lines, to emphasize what the popes have said in regard
to the worker.*

*But there were also criticisms to make as to the acceptance by the
unions of the industrial set-up as it was, private enterprise, competition, and industrial capitalism.*

*Frankly, our position was that we had better work against the
whole order—work for decentralization, in some cases even for abolition of the machine and the assembly line where it definitely went
against the best interests of man and his needs and his nature.*

By the end of the thirties, Day had come closer to Peter
Maurin's point of view, and as a result some members of the
Catholic Worker who were attracted to the movement for its
labor activism separated and formed the Association of Catholic
Trade Unionists. As Day reflects on the Catholic Worker position
on labor she reveals Maurin's influence on her:

*Since the unions were organized more for wages and hours,
rather than for mutual aid and indoctrination, very often what we
had to offer in the way of a program did not interest them. Our point
of view was foreign if not hostile at times. Often it is a matter of
criticism that we have not continued to work with unions as we did
in 1933 through 1938. Frankly, it was because we were not interested in increasing armaments, big business, perpetuating the status
quo, and working in many cases perhaps toward state ownership.*

*We must continue to protest injustices, bad working conditions,
and poor wages which are general now in the face of the high cost of
living; but our vision is of another system, another social order, a
state of society where, as Marx and Engels put it, "Each man works
according to his ability and receives according to his need." Or as St.
Paul put it, "Let your abundance supply their want." Men are beginning to think of the annual wage, in the unions, but not the family
wage. Usually it is "equal pay for equal work." But that holy pope,
Pius XI, said we should work to de-proletarize the worker, to get him*

out of the wage-earning class and into the propertied class, so that he would own his own home, as well as his tools.

We must continue to get out into the highways and byways to distribute the paper even if it is not the food the man in the street wants. Religion is morbid to most people, and indeed it is a matter of dying to self, in order to live for God and one's neighbor. Religion has too long been the opium of the people. I forgot how the jingle in the first issue of Integrity *ran, but the sense of it was this:*

John Smith puts on his hat and goes to church on Sunday,

And John Smith goes to hell for what he does on Monday.

Not Saturday night mind you, when he may be taking surcease from care in some tavern, but for the work he engages in whether it is in the advertising business, or a fat job in the rubber company, or copper or nickel mines, or a steamship company. We participate in the sin of others; we are all helping to make the kind of world that makes for war.

Yes, let us get out into Union Square, along Forty-second Street, in front of Madison Square Garden and distribute and sell The Catholic Worker. *We have been doing that for many years, but we need to do much more of it. As the older ones get tired (and Stanley has become a tired radical in this job of selling the paper) let the younger students and workers take over the job of being fools for Christt.*[3] *One seminarian sold the paper all summer for us. One rainy night when we were going into a CIO meeting, there he was standing in the downpour shouting, "Read* The Catholic Worker— *the only thing that isn't all wet!"*

Big Dan used to call out (in opposition to Communist salesmen, who shouted, "Read The Daily Worker"), *"Read* The Catholic Worker *daily."*

Leaflets, pamphlets, papers, as well as more scholarly journals, are needed to reach the man in the street. Many an apostle has been found selling Catholic literature on the street corner, and has been queried as to his positions and beliefs and has had to begin to study, "to know the reason for the faith that is in him," in order to answer all the questions that are put to him. And many a time he just can't answer them and it's no use his trying.

While writing of the early days of the movement Day reflects on the enthusiasm and the meaning it all had for certain people, including herself.

To reach the masses through the spiritual and corporal works of mercy was our goal. Of course getting Catholic literature around is performing quite a few of those tasks. It is "enlightening the igno-rant" and "counseling the doubtful," "comforting the afflicted," and you might even say that walking a picket line is doing these things too, as well as "rebuking the sinner." When we talk of the works of mercy, we usually think of feeding the hungry, clothing the naked, and sheltering the homeless. Some grow disillusioned with this less romantic work. But we have had to do them all, even burying the dead. One does not necessarily have to establish, run, or live in a House of Hospitality, as Peter named the hospices we have running around the country, in order to practice the works of mercy. The early Fathers of the Church said that every house should have a Christ room. But it is generally only the poorest who are hospitable. A young college graduate hitchhiking across the country during the Depression (he was trying to make up his mind about his vocation) said that the only place he found hospitality was among the Negroes and the Mexicans. Certainly priests' housekeepers did not extend any. He met so much misery and starvation that when he reached Los Angeles, he finally started a House of Hospitality there and in that house he met with so many impossible cases that he turned more and more to the spiritual weapons, and now he is a priest, with the most powerful weapons of all in his hands.

Every house should have a Christ room. The coat that hangs in your closet belongs to the poor. If your brother comes to you hungry and you say, "Go, be thou filled," what kind of hospitality is that? It is no use turning people away to an agency, to the city or the state or Catholic Charities. It is you yourself who must perform the works of mercy. Often you can only give the price of a meal, or a bed on the Bowery. Often you can only hope that it will be spent for that. Often you can literally take off a garment, if it only be a scarf, and warm some shivering brother. But personally, at a personal sacrifice, these were the ways, Peter used to insist, to combat the growing tendency on the part of the state to take over. This is the job that Our Lord gave us to do. "Inasmuch as you have done it unto one of the least of my brethren, you have done it unto me."

The paper inspired by Maurin and produced by Day launched a movement that grew rapidly through the Depression years of the 1930s. On the eve of World War II there were Catholic Worker Houses of Hospitality in every major city in the United States, and over a dozen farms, where enthusiastic followers, mostly young college graduates, were trying to work out Peter Maurin's philosophy of personalism. For the first time in the history of American Catholicism the words "Catholic thought" were being interjected into conversations regarding racism, anti-Semitism, workers' rights, and social justice for the poor. Enthusiasts promoted the *Catholic Worker* because it represented an idea that stood as a contrast to the materialist philosophies of capitalism and communism, which they rejected equally. Day reflected on this growth and its meaning:

A few months later, my brother moved to a small town to be an editor of a paper, and I started the Catholic Worker, *turning the apartment into an office. The poor of the neighborhood began to come in, and we began to make their problems our own. Some of them came to live with us. There was the Armenian anarchist who wrote poetry. There was the French teacher from Montreal. There was the German carpenter who loved discussion as much as Peter did. We had to rent an additional apartment for men and one for women within the year. It was in 1936 that one of our readers offered us the use of 115 Mott Street, where we are now.*

Families in the neighborhood who were being evicted came to get our help in moving, and we borrowed horse and wagon and push-cart, and the help of the neighborhood, and helped people move, and saw first hand the actual destitution there was behind the closed doors all around us. Why did people have to live so?

Marquette University Archives

As Day points out, Peter's response was that people did not "have to live so." The answer for Maurin was the land.

Peter's excerpts on the land movement gained more weight with us every day, though what impact we are going to make on a city of seven million we do not know. At the same time that he brought these notes on the land, a chapter a day synopsized, he brought a series of quotations from Fr. Bede Jarret, trying to meet the objections of our godless friends, who asked the ancient question, "How can you worship a God who allows such suffering?" In his Easy Essay form Peter wrote:

> *In his Summa Theologica*
> *St. Thomas Aquinas allows only two*
> *possible objections to the existence of God.*
> *And one of these is the existence of evil.*
>
> *How can we, he suggests, suppose God to be omnipotent,*
> *if we find things in this world that spoil His plan;*
> *and if God is not omnipotent,*
> *how can He be God at all?*
>
> *The answer of St. Thomas can be very briefly given*
> *for it is nothing else than a quotation from*
> *Saint Augustine.*
>
> *If evil and sin, says Saint Augustine, spoilt the*
> *plan of God,*
> *He would clearly not be omnipotent and would not be God.*
> *But if He is so powerful*
> *that He can make even sin*
> *fit into the working out of His design,*
> *then the whole objection fails.*
> *Out of evil He brings forth good.*

This quotation Peter had hopefully presented to the poor who lost their faith. "Why bring that up?" is probably what they thought, but their courtesy getting the better of them they listened with attentive respect and cordiality as one must always listen to a benefactor.

"But perhaps this will make it clearer," Peter went on to explain, reading aloud from his vantage point in the middle of the floor.

To see what it means
we must first of all remember the old truth
that the mysteries of God are above reason.

Therefore it is as well to begin
by insisting that there is no answer.
And the religion that would suppose
that it had at least discovered the way through
would stand itself condemned.

But granting all this,
there is still much that a Catholic can see
to help him bear patiently
the evils of this present life.

He went on reading to us, but realizing that we were perhaps more intent on the eviction that was impending, he pressed the pages of quotations upon us to read at our leisure.

It was inconceivable to Peter that anyone should be uninterested. That is part of the secret of his charm and of his success. He had a gentle insistence and enthusiastic generosity, an assumption that one was intellectually capable of grasping the most profound truths and was honestly ready to change one's life to conform thereby.

I have seen him buttonhole an acquaintance on a street corner, engage a casual friend in conversation, start propounding to casual acquaintances in coffee shops; and being no respecter of persons, though of course with a recognition of hierarchy and spheres of influence, he was quite happy talking to workers on the Bowery as to bishops. Peter came out too with the rest of the neighbors to help protest against the evictions and move the family to other quarters.

Marquette University Archives

Peter Maurin's world of Catholic social theory became for Dorothy Day a practical plan of social action. Yet, as she admitted in her biography of Maurin, she remained nonplussed by many of the man's actions. But she proceeded with those parts of his program she did understand (Houses of Hospitality, farming communes, and the paper) and these have become the hallmarks of the Catholic Worker as it continues to exist today. In the following section, however, she admits that there was much of Maurin's plan that was never realized.

Let it be conceded right away, before going any further, that I do not pretend to understand Peter Maurin. I can use that as an excuse now for the incoherence of this account. To me, my account of him may seem clear and well worked out, but to the reader, especially to those readers who have not come in contact with the Catholic Worker and know nothing of our way of life, this whole story of the man may seem disjointed, irrelevant, a patchwork.

We do not understand ourselves. In trying to write an account of my own conversion in From Union Square to Rome, *I was overcome again and again by the fear of misrepresenting, of not being truthful, of ascribing to myself motives that years back were not truly the influences that worked upon me.*

If we do not understand ourselves, nor those nearest to us, those we love, those of our family, then it is easy to say right now that I do not understand Peter Maurin. I do not understand, for instance, why he talks about the things he does to the people he does. Why, for instance, given an opportunity to talk to a group of striking seamen, during the 1937 waterfront strike, should he pick out the subject of André Gide and his reactions to Soviet Russia, and discourse on that for two hours? Perhaps he recognized a Communist in the audience and spoke only to him.

Then there is his plan, which I must confess I did not understand, to popularize the scholars. He wanted to pick out one hundred European exiles, whom he called traditionalists, interview them, get digests of their message, which in turn, he would bring to the colum-

nists to popularize, so that they, in turn, could bring them to the men of action, the men of action being politicians.

Peter said, "The men of action don't think, and the men who think, don't act." So he would begin with Tillisch, the symbolist, Westbrook Pegler, the columnist, and James Farley, the politician. (This was a plan in 1939.) What they might have in common, what effect Tillisch's thought might have on Farley's action was hard to say. But when Farley was approached with Tillisch's ideas on symbolism, he was doubtless going to be surprised and perhaps moved to action, such as politely throwing Peter's emissaries out of his office. For Peter entrusted these ventures to emissaries, in this case to Arthur Sheehan, Carl Bauer, and Marjorie Crowe. Once having conceived the idea, got the ball rolling, so to speak, he could meditate on a new idea, launch a new project. This one never got further than Tillisch.

Then there was his idea of the troubadours for Christ, five of them preferably, who would go about the country from city to city begging their way, chanting the praises of God and the rebuilding of the social order. In order to cover this vast country, Peter was quite content to use a machine, a car and a trailer. After all, a car, a typewriter, a sewing machine, is the extension of the hand of man and can be controlled, and so does not enslave man. The idea was delightful, I conceded, if only Peter did not take the best workers from Mott Street. Of course, there was the expense, though not for us, of supporting five troubadours on the road. We could not use the money sent in for the House of Hospitality or bread line for such a project. Peter admitted that, but neither did I believe that our friends and readers would supply five healthy appetites with food and car and trailer with gas. It seemed too much to expect. So the idea of the five troubadours never was worked out. Perhaps some time it will be. The car and trailer, of course, remain a problem.

The very naked simplicity of Peter's schemes provokes thought, as well as astonishment. Certainly conflicts result from his ideas. How many a conflict, for instance, over that little phrase—"Workers should be scholars and scholars workers."

There are phrases that still throw the leaders of the movement all over the country into a furor, especially on the farms where the family idea and the community idea or personalist and communitarian ideas are and always will be in conflict. These phrases are simple ones but packed with dynamite. "Fire the Bosses!" "Work four hours daily!" "Eat what you raise, and raise what you eat!" "Love God and do as you please!" That last, in case our reader doesn't recognize it, is St. Augustine's, but the rest are Peter's.

Peter loved to fling out catchy slogans, and then watch the fur fly. On every farming commune, in every House of Hospitality, the conflict has gone on for years.

"It makes for clarification of thought," said Peter happily.

The discussion has gone on for so long that other groups started still another conflict, not over the fundamental ideas themselves, which were still anything but clarified—ideas on authority and freedom, personalism and communitarianism—but a conflict on the "meaning of meaning." Peter's slogans were held up to ridicule as catch words and clichés, and instead of seeking the meaning, the banal was held up as a warning, and the oversensitive dropped from the conflict, afraid of ridicule, and the persevering and intent sought for new ways of stating the old conflict, which began when Christ propounded the truth to his disciples and "Those who could take, took it," and "Many went away sorrowing, for it was a hard saying."

"The truth must be restated every twenty years," Peter kept quoting Ibsen.

"There can be no revolution without a theory of revolution," he quoted Lenin.

And these ideas, so agonizingly and painfully worked out in our living with others on farms and in communities in town, are the theory of the Green Revolution that Peter talks about.

Reading over these last pages, the juxtaposition of Mr. Farley and Mr. Tillisch does not seem so mad, or am I so under the spell of Peter that I am uncritical? Perhaps it smacks too much of the digest, the outline idea—getting the thought of a hundred scholars to bring to a hundred columnists, to popularize with a hundred politicians. But the fundamental truth is there. We have been betrayed by the intellectuals of the past. We need to be set right by the intellectuals of the present. We need to study in order to love and act. The way Peter put it is this:

> Pope Pius IX and Cardinal Newman
> consider liberalism
> whether it be
> religious, philosophic, or economic,
> the greatest error of the nineteenth century.
>
> Modern liberalism
> is the logical sequence
> of the so-called age of Enlightenment—
> the age of Voltaire, Rousseau, Thomas Paine—
> sometimes called the Age of Reason
> in opposition to the Age of Faith.
>
> By sponsoring nationalism and capitalism
> modern liberals
> have given up the search for truth
> and have become paid propagandists.
>
> So the Age of Reason
> has become the Age of Treason,
> as Julien Benda points out
> in his book entitled
> "The Treason of the Intellectuals."

Most followers of the Catholic Worker movement agree with Day that outside the Houses of Hospitality and the paper there was little that was practically applicable in Maurin's vision. However there were people apparently as far away from Maurin's thought as Roosevelt's "Brain Trust" who shared Maurin's vision

of a world of art and artists, which would interpret and human-
ize the harsh social conflicts of the decade. One example of confluence between New Deal thought and Maurin's was the
government's "Four Arts program." Of the initial $2 billion
appropriation for the Works Progress Administration (WPA),
designed to provide work for some of the millions of unemployed, $27 million was earmarked for unemployed artists,
actors, musicians, and writers. During its existence the Four Arts
program at its peak employed over forty thousand musicians,
artists, writers, and actors.[4] Of course the bulk of WPA money
went to provide basic jobs that could somehow be identified as
promoting the public good. However, fixed within the legislation
was an attempt to remedy a problem noted by personalists—that
work in a capitalist system had denied the person "his true daily
bread: the development of an interior life in the heart of communitarian life. Such a life would initiate aesthetic improve-
ments as well," the personalists pointed out, and "Art must
become once again mixed with the day to day life of everyone."[5]
Programs such as the National Recovery Act (NRA) and the WPA
demonstrate that within the New Deal there were people with
influence who wanted to move away from the classic models of
capitalism toward a more human and personalist economy.

The NRA and the Artists projects demonstrate a confluence
of New Deal and Catholic Worker personalist philosophy, but
the clearest and most concrete example of harmony between the
economic vision of some New Dealers and Peter Maurin is provided by the New Deal's rural farm legislation.

Despite its urban roots, a "back-to-the-land movement"
always remained central to Maurin's plan. He did not believe
that the industrial capitalist system would ever have the capacity to support the entire workforce, and Franklin Roosevelt
agreed with this observation. The president felt that even if the
recovery of production reached the peak levels of 1929, there
would still be unemployment in the cities.[6] Arthur Schlesinger
points out that Roosevelt felt very strongly about striking a bet-

ter balance between urban and rural population, and a balance between subsistence farming and part-time factory work. Before his inauguration, Roosevelt spoke privately of putting a million families back on the land and into subsistence farming. During his first months in office he told Senator George Norris, "I would like . . . a bill which would . . . allow us to spend $25 million this year to put 25,000 families on farms at an average cost of $1,000 a family." He asked Norris to talk it over with some of "our other dreamers" on Capitol Hill. Apparently there were enough dreamers, since Congress appropriated $25 million for what Senator Bankhead of Alabama called the model for a "new basis of American society."[7]

In the precarious economic world of the thirties, many people dreamed of a new postcapitalist economic structure. It was an environment that allowed practical government bureaucrats to call themselves dreamers and dreamers such as the Catholic Workers to call themselves realists. But soon the era of experimentation and dreaming ended. The terrible and threatening reality of fascism overshadowed all dreams of social economic redemption. The United States, along with the rest of the world, felt the terrible threat of Adolf Hitler and his Nazis, who had appropriated just enough of the idealism of the thirties to hypnotize an entire generation of people desperately searching for community and economic security. Hitler distorted the ideal of universal community and transmogrified it into a racist and paranoid fascist state, which promised economic security based on a world of German masters and Russian slaves. Clearly, Hitler's fascist state represented the most horrible threat to civilization in human memory.

Many New Dealers who had been earnestly searching for alternatives to liberal capitalism had to abandon their dreams as it became obvious to them that only liberal capitalist democracy, with all its faults, represented a system that could successfully challenge the Nazi threat. World War II effectively ended the influence of personalist ideas in political America. John Cogley, a Catholic Worker radical in the thirties who turned into a post-war liberal, acknowledged that it was the harsh reality of fascism that brought an end to the idealism of the thirties.[8] James Farrell has pointed out that personalism as an idea returned after the war but only on the margins of American thought.[9] Even before the war, the Catholic Worker noted that the heady days of radicals influencing government decision makers were over. In a front-page editorial in February 1939 the *Catholic Worker* reported that they could no longer support New Deal policies, especially in the area of foreign affairs. "It is a painful duty to criticize one [Roosevelt] whom we have learned to love for his sense of charity and whom we have learned to respect for the wonderful way in which he handled the internal affairs of the country during its most trying economic years," the editors lamented, but a break with the Catholic Worker had become inevitable due to the President's belligerent European policy.

As war became inevitable, Catholic Worker personalism drew that movement further from the mainstream and into a very narrow channel of pacifism. Taking this path split the Catholic Worker, and drove it out of its precarious place on the edge of the mainstream of American political thought. After the war, personalism, which had reached its most influential political hearing during the early New Deal era, would settle into the fringes of the intellectual tradition in this country.

5

Life with Peter

ॐ

What we do for our brother
for Christ's sake
is what we carry with us
when we die.
              —Peter Maurin

It was Saturday afternoon and Peter came up to my room in *Martha House, as we called the woman's House of Hospitality, when the opera was on [the radio]. I had missed the opening explanation; there was nothing about Alceste[1] in the opera guide, and Peter stayed through the first and second intermissions—so I never did know what the opera was about. The music was rather melancholy, high and plaintive, with not much variety in tone. Or so it seemed to me, just from hearing it while Peter talked and I replied, made notes, and read his essays and looked up letters to show him and get his comment.*

Peter knew my weakness for music. I remember one night on Fifteenth Street, John [Dorothy's brother] was at work and Tamar [her daughter] was in bed with the measles. Tessa [John's wife] and I were most anxious to hear the symphony. I think it was Tchaikovsky's Pathetique. But Peter was there. He was instructing me, tutoring me in history, one might say. Tessa had a gift for listening. She was one of those harsh Spanish beauties. She always listened to Peter with rapt attention, and with respectful agreement. She never did agree with him [ed. note: Both Tessa and her husband, Dorothy's brother, were Communists]. She had a Spanish gift for hospitality, which meant that she listened, she admired, she assented in respectful politeness. She was going to have baby, and her swelling body made her more full and soft and sweet. Mike Gold [an old Communist friend] used to come around often and with Jewish fervor look at her admiringly and say, "Why does everyone love pregnant women?"

Peter always overestimated people's capacity for learning. His indoctrination might begin at three o'clock in the afternoon, but by nine, one was ready to listen to music. But Peter is a Frenchman, with a French mind. There were problems to be settled, plans to be made, ideas to be thrashed out, and clarification of thought to be achieved. It was hard to keep him quiet for an hour.

We begged him. "Peter, a symphony! Just an hour! Do sit quietly."

He did his best, but sooner or later, his face would start working, his eyes light up, his nose twitch, his finger begin to mark out points in the air before him. Usually he'd take out a notebook and start jotting points.

Finally, when he could not bear it any longer, he'd look at me wistfully, and then, seeing my adamant expression, would turn to Tessa. I remember that night especially because he went over and knelt down by her chair and began whispering to her, unable to restrain himself longer. Peter liked singing folk songs, but he was decidedly not interested in symphonies or operas.

Now, this afternoon he had come up to tell me about seeing Fr. Orchard. "He wants you to come and see him," he stated.

"You can arrange it. Go see two or three people at once. Yesterday I saw three people, Carleton Hayes, Fr. Orchard, and Jean Kennedy. I was giving them my outline of history. Carleton Hayes being a historian, I wanted to read it to him, and then I read it to his wife, and after that I took it to Fr. Orchard and read it to him, and then I went to see Jean Kennedy. She is a convert (that's right, she is your godchild) and so she is interested in getting a Catholic point of view. The trouble with people is they do not study history. Statistics show that people are not studying history in colleges, as *they used to. We need to understand how things became as they are, in order to act now so as to change the future."*

"Here! Read this! How do you like this arrangement?" Peter was always trying new arrangements and groupings for his essays. He enjoyed getting things neatly lined up, in place and simplified for people on the run.

As he once said, he did not start to write until he got tired of trying to make people listen to him. Yet one cannot imagine Peter in a classroom, or other than he is, a peripatetic teacher and historian, trying to reach the man on the street, the man on the park bench.

I enjoyed sitting and reading that afternoon, while the snow fell softly outside and the windows rattled in the wind, the hard-coal fire burned in the grate, and the opera came over the radio. But as the wind increased in volume, I began to think of my daughter, who had gone down to the farm for the weekend. Maryfarm is at Easton, Pennsylvania, seventy-five miles away from New York.

It is a straight road, from our very door, across Canal Street, through the Holland Tunnel under the Hudson River, and then along Route 22 to Easton, and two miles beyond on the banks of the Delaware River, two miles below the point in Easton where the Lehigh pours over a small dam into the shallow Delaware.

As we sat so secure, storm warnings began to come over the radio of increased snow, wind, and ice on the highways, and I mentioned my worry to Peter.

"But it will make her sturdy," he said reassuringly. And he went on to quote D'Annunzio. At that point, two old streetwalkers in the next room began having a loud argument, and there was a terrific blare from the radio and I missed it. I began to hear again when he was talking about trees. "The wind is as good as the sun," he was saying. "The pine trees in the valley may be very beautiful to the eye with their wide-spreading branches, but those on the mountainsides that have their roots imbedded into rocks and have to be always stretching to reach the sun, and get much of the wind as a consequence—they are the ones that are useful and make good lumber." He dismissed my worries and picked up from my desk a leaflet put out by Gorham Munson on social credit.

"When he started sending out those leaflets, he advised his recipients that he was sending them to thirty leading minds of the country."

"A raw piece of flattery to induce them to read," I told him.

But Peter brushed this aside. "This is what we too must do, to bring the thought of the scholars to the columnists to bring to the common man. We will pick out the leading thinkers—"

"But we will be guilty of flattery too—"

"No," Peter replied, "they may not be thinking right, but I mean the popular thinkers, the 'key' men who are quoted and who are accepted as leaders in thought, even though they may be bad leaders."

And he picked up another letter from the desk, from President McCracken of Vassar, and continued, "Now here they are talking about this luncheon of the National Conference of Christians and Jews given for 118 American writers. Of this number only a few attended, I see. Archibald McLeish, John P. Marquand, Muriel Rukeyser, Carl Van Doren, Thornton Wilder. . . . And you. Now you get all the rest of the names and we will send material to them on personalism. Send them the Catholic Worker first until they get used to that."

"Will they ever get used to it?"

Peter had far more patience than I have. Or rather I should say he had far more patience with the intellectual, the college man. He had not so much patience with the worker.

Acting as if I had not interrupted he continued right on with his ideas.

"We must get all the material from Paulding—he is literary editor of Commonweal now—and he will give us more detailed stuff about the leading personalists of France. There is Mounier, editor of L'Esprit, whose Personalist Manifesto was translated by Virgil Michel. There is a Davidson or Dennison, I cannot remember his name. He is a historian. There is Landberg, a psychologist, and Jacques Madaule, who ran for police chief in Paris. He was running for office as an opportunity to make his points on the pluralist state. Not that he thought he would get the office. He is not a politician. These Catholic philosophers have encyclopedic minds. Agnostics have specialists' minds.

"*But we have got to further the idea of personalist pluralism. The word 'democracy' has been overworked. Personalist pluralism is difficult but there is nothing else to express the idea.*

"*There is an entire chapter in Maritain's* True Humanism *on pluralism and there is a definition of personalist democracy, which is quite different from the majority-rule idea.*"

Peter's ideas on personalism have been and are hard to clarify or popularize. When Hazen Ordway, down on the Easton Farm, was asked what his ideas were in regard to personalism, what personalism meant to him, he too quoted, "Love God and do as you please." Many of those on the farm will say, "Personalism means, 'Fire the bosses.' Everyone is his own boss. Everyone does what he thinks best." Which is what they wish to think.

The idea of leadership, the idea of authority, has never been clarified, so personalism degenerates into anarchy. With conflicts in the movement Peter always got back to the fundamental problem—the necessity of knowing something about what he called the "art of human contacts."

Getting off the subject for a moment this afternoon, Peter suggested that we take a young child down on the farm who was having home difficulties, and turn him over to one of the families.

"*But in the first place," I objected, "the mother will not want to part with him, and in the second place, I don't think our family down there will manage any better. They are pretty much in a fog about voluntary poverty, and about the craft idea. They think poverty means a barren house, a complete absence of beauty. Really, I believe it is because they can't manage for themselves. They don't know how to run a house, and so they justify themselves by talking about poverty. But a room can be made beautiful with a few flowers, plants, a bookcase, and curtains at clean windows. And outdoors, the rural fence John Griffin made is broken down, and things scattered about a good deal. They don't seem to see these things. They do not seem to have the gift of homemaking. And so they do not set a good example to the migratory family.*"

"*But I will take those jobs!" Peter said eagerly. "I will take the* job this spring of straightening the place up, keeping things looking good. They will learn that way. And this year, instead of breaking rocks in the hot sun, I'm going to the spring between the two farms and break that pile of rocks there. Then John Fillinger can bring the horses up and get a load and fix the road, as it is needed. I'll always have an extra hammer by my side, and when anyone wants to help, I'll just hand him a hammer."

"And I'll bet there'll be a great many round-table discussions up on the hillside, in the cool shade."

A few summers ago Peter took as his job the road mending and rock crushing. I remembered one fellow who used to sit out under the trees and watch Peter work. Peter always carried his point so far that he would never ask anyone to help him to do a job.

"People that come to the farm should come because they want to work. That is to be understood. They must see the necessity and the beauty of work and do it. They must not be told. It must be voluntary. They are not working for their board and bed. They are working as a free contribution to the farming commune."

But Jim used to say, "I'll work when I'm told to. I want someone to give me orders." So he used to sit under the tree and do nothing all day. I do not think he was very happy in this attitude. We used to blame it on his German mind. We could understand his point of view too, and he had a stubbornness to make his point, and go on sitting under a tree.

But Peter never gave an order. He would sacrifice material success any day in order to drive home his ideas in regard to personalism.

Of his little essays we all like those on "Gentle Personalism," and although we never tire of quoting such essays, I'm afraid we do not live up to them very well.

Personalist Communitarianism

A personalist
is a go-giver
not a go-getter.

He tries to give
what he has
and does not
try to get
what the other fellow has.

He tries to be good
by doing good
to the other fellow.

He is other-centered
not self-centered.
He has a social doctrine
of the common good.

He spreads the social doctrine
of the common good
through words and deeds.

He speaks through deeds
as well as words.

Through words and deeds
he brings into existence
a common unity,
the common unity
of a community.

Better and Better Off

The world would be better off
if people tried
to become better.

And people would become better
if they stopped trying
to be better off.

For when everybody tries
to become better off
nobody is better off.

But when everybody tries
to become better
everybody is better off.

Everybody would be rich
if nobody tried
to become richer.

And nobody would be poor
if everybody tried
to be the poorest.

And everybody would be
what he ought to be
if everybody tried to be
what he wants
the other fellow to be.

Peter was always getting back to St. Francis of Assisi, who was most truly the "gentle personalist." In his poverty, rich; in renouncing all, possessing all; generous, giving out of the fullness of his heart, sowing generously and reaping generously, humble and asking when in need, possessing freedom and all joy.

Without doubt, Peter was a free and joyous person. And it was the freedom and joyousness that came from a clear heart and soul. There are those who spoke of his anarchistic nature, because of his refusal to enter into political controversy, his refusal to use worldly means to change the social order. He does not refuse to use material means, physical means, secular means, the means that are at hand. But the means of expediency that men have turned to for so many ages, he disdains. He is no diplomat, no politician. He has so thoroughly discouraged in his followers the use of political means that he has been termed an anarchist by many, especially by our dear Jesuit friend, Father Fowling, who has often come to us and talked to us of proportional representation.

To give up superfluous possession! Peter had no income so he did not worry about income taxes. He used those things he needed, in the way of clothing and food, "as though he used them not." He had no worries about style, fit, or fashion. He ate what was put before him, and if he preferred anything he preferred vegetable stews to meat, a hot drink to a cold, olive oil to butter. He did not smoke, he did not drink wine only "because it causes his brother to stumble." Otherwise, he believed in feasts as well as fasts, and there are after all many feast days, days of rejoicing, weddings, baptismal feasts, name days, and all the saints' days.

Saint Francis desired that men should work with their hands. Peter enjoyed manual labor. He used to tell Fr. Virgil Michel that if Benedictines had kept to their early ideal of manual labor, there would not be so many breakdowns from mental overwork. "We must use the whole man," says Peter, "so that we may be holy men." He might have been quoting—it sounds like Eric Gill, but it also sounds like Peter.

Nothing he liked better than building fires and getting down and poking the grate until it was all but out. And poking kindling wood in under the coals, and shaking it down, and finally dumping it, and rebuilding it all together—that was fun. Then he would laboriously go over the coal (we have no sifters) getting out the pieces of unburned coal so none would be wasted. Then he would empty the ashes—and usually the wind blew them all over Peter, turning his hair, his old suit and shoes gray.

I have seen him setting out like that, to give a lecture somewhere, all unbrushed and uncombed, and have run after him to refurbish him a bit for company. "It is for the sake of others," I told him.

But Peter was oblivious to appearances. There was not much in the way of manual labor he could do around Mott Street excepting help keep the fires going and mending chairs. We are always short of chairs, so each one is a treasure. Ours is a neighborhood where people live out-of-doors, a good part of winter as well as summer. The women in the tenement on either side of us, back and front, come down on the sidewalk when their work in the house is done, and just sit. Usually they come into the store, which is the office, and take the chairs. If they like the chairs, they bring them upstairs with them to their homes, leaving us the old broken ones.

"That is the way the poor are treated," I told Peter. "How long does it take Christianity to work anyway?" Because of our generosity in letting them borrow our chairs—because we believe that when someone takes our coat we should offer him our cloak too, then the argument is, "They do not appreciate good things, they don't value what they have—so we might as well take them. We'll take care of them." I've seen the argument working in people's minds hundreds of times. They justify themselves cleverly. "The poor don't know the difference," they say. "Them as has gits," and from them who have not, what they have shall be taken away. That's us. They leave us the broken-down chairs, or those too heavy to be moved, and Peter mends them uncomplaining.

On the farming commune, there was plenty of work for all, another reason why Peter was always extolling the land. People could not live without working. Work was as necessary as bread. But what was needed was a philosophy of labor. Work was a gift, a vocation. Before the Fall Adam was given the garden to cultivate. It was only after the Fall that all nature travailed and groaned so that man also had to work with the sweat of his brow and combat earthquakes, floods, droughts, boll weevils, Japanese beetles, fatigue, and sloth. We have to recognize work as a penance, but we must also recognize work as a gift. Man has talents which God has given him, and he must develop these talents. He must find the work he can do best, and then learn to do it well, for his own sake and the sake of his fellows.

Peter's indoctrination about scholars and workers had this practical result around the houses of hospitality and farming commune. When the scholar started scrubbing and cleaning house, the cooperation from the worker was more willing, more spontaneous. Everyone wanted to help. And the labor and exercise tended to relieve the discouragement that often tended to bog down the scholar. He understood better the discouragements of the poor, his slothfulness, and his *hopelessness. He began, too, to understand what Christ meant when he said he came to minister, not to be ministered unto. He began to understand the humiliations of the very poor and by seeking them voluntarily he found peace and rest in them. "My yoke is easy and my burden light." "The meek shall inherit the earth." But these things are not understood until practiced. As St. Francis said, "You cannot know what you have not practiced."*

A Jewish convert, who had been making a retreat with us at Maryfarm, said some weeks after, "It is hard to live in the upside-down world of the Gospels." Truly it is a world of paradoxes, giving up one's life in order to save it, dying to live. It is truly voluntary poverty, stripping oneself even of what the world calls dignity, human respect.

For truly it must be admitted that one does not always have the respect of the poor, of the workers. Take Smitty, for instance. He gave out clothes in the basement storeroom every day, and for three hours he took the abuse of women and men who came for underwear and socks and sweaters and coats.

"These clothes are sent in here for us!" they would scream at him. "You're holding out on us! You gave it to him yesterday and now you have nothing for me! You're selling the stuff yourself!" Smitty meekly accepted it all. He was in rags himself, down at the heel, wearing his clothes until we begged him to find something else in order to wash the things he had on. He was so poor, and looked so poor, that the miserable ones who came suspected him of their own vices. He must drink, he must steal—it is beyond reason that anyone voluntarily should stay down in that dingy rat-ridden hole, under the five-story tenement and give out clothes and bits of literature, and keep on taking abuse as meekly as he did.

Already he had been up since five o'clock in the morning, getting the coffee ready for the bread line, slicing bread, heavy pumpernickel and rye, which the men soak in their coffee. There are three or four hundred every morning. There used to be twice that number, but now it is a time of "full employment" and there are not as many transients, so many unemployed. There are the old, the crippled, and the unemployables in the neighborhood. They are served in one of the two stores which front our Saint Joseph's House of Hospitality in New York. The store is long and narrow, and there is not enough room for tables and chairs. The men must come in on a line, be served their coffee and bread at a counter, drink it and eat their soaked-up bread, and then go back on the line again and take their turn on second helpings, and they can take all the bread they wish in their ragged pockets.

Smitty had other helpers of course, all part of our family. There was Alex, the Russian, who was torpedoed in the last war and afloat for hours. There was a little Swiss fellow, very critical of the men he was serving. There was old Bill, whose reputation was such that we had to watch the faucets and the plumbing to see that he did not walk off with them. Every time he saw me, he grabbed a broom and looked very useful. A few times, after especially flagrant thefts, he was told to go, but he found a way to get around us. He took up his abode on the sidewalk across the street, and late at night we would see him sitting there, until finally we were worn down and told him to go upstairs and sleep there. If the house was crowded, and there was no bed, the floor was better than the street

One recognizes how fundamentally Christian these ideas are when one sees the reaction of such a friend as Kichi Harada, who is not a Christian but a Buddhist. Miss Harada was a lecturer and artist. She taught until some nine years ago and then when her money was exhausted she came to us, and lived with us until her death. At first she looked upon the other women in the house as menials, as the hewers of wood and the drawers of water. We have no bath and no hot water, so Miss Harada had to heat her pail of water in the kitchen and carry it up four flights of stairs. She liked to take baths at such strange hours as two o'clock in the morning, and many a time I was awakened to the banging of pots and pans above my head. She distrusted our laundries and when the sheets were returned, she used to scald them anew and hang them out to dry. And for all the water that she used, she asked me to use my authority to have the other women in the house wait upon her, to carry it for her. But there was no one who was willing to carry Miss Harada's water for her, and, of course, I did not ask them. It would be a following of Christian principles for me to carry her water, but I could not ask others to do so.

When I washed dishes in the evening (the women took turns) Miss Harada used to protest in her deep voice, "But this is not for you to do. This is for others." But she took to seizing a dish towel to help me, and after we had conversed on the subject of scholars and workers, and leaders and servants, the ministers and the ministered, she took to doing her share of the dishwashing, very sturdily.

Once she cooked a feast for us that will go down in the history of the Catholic Worker. We like to celebrate name days around the Catholic Worker hospices as well as birthdays and baptismal days, and Miss Harada wanted a name day for herself. So we gave her the feast of St. Francis Xavier, the Apostle to Japan. His feast day comes in December, near the tragic date of Pearl Harbor. She had planned for weeks, and I do not think that Pearl Harbor had anything to do with the near collapse of her feast. Getting the money from the office, she did the shopping herself, buying Chinese vegetables and meat and the needed sauces. Filled with the sense of holiday, she came home early in the afternoon to start her preparations. The kitchen in Maryhouse (our women's house) then was on the third floor, while Miss Harada's room was on the fifth. Putting the food on the kitchen table, she went on up to her room to change her dress and get an apron. Her step was unmistakable, firm and heavy. One of the other women in the house who occasionally takes to the bottle (after a half day of housecleaning in the neighborhood) heard her step and betook herself to the kitchen. I happened to be in my room, just below the kitchen, and heard the disturbance, which began almost immediately. With horrid curses directed at "that Jap who was going to poison us all, the dirty yellow b—," Miss L began hurling meat and vegetables all over the room.

My heart started to pound with righteous wrath. (Righteous anger is all right, provided there is no undue desire for revenge, St. Thomas says. But whatever he says, I know it is a most disturbing emotion.) I wanted to belabor Miss L. As it was, I was able to make my way to the kitchen and order her most firmly and sternly to her room, assisting her up the stairs so that she would surely get there before Miss Harada came down again. Her knowledge that I was in the house would keep her out of the kitchen, I thought hopefully.

Miss Harada came blithely down shortly after and started her preparation of the feast. I was morose the rest of the afternoon, stewing and fretting within myself (in my righteous wrath). Everything would be spoiled! Miss L would come to dinner and continue her cursing! And here was company coming in, a governess and a little girl who wanted to visit the Catholic Worker and see what a House of Hospitality was like.

The afternoon passed. We finally sat down to a crowded board, and Miss L swayed and swaggered into the room, anxious to be of service (she usually is first assistant in the kitchen), weaving her way in and out, helping to wait on the table, passing boiling hot food dangerously close to our guests, and humming through it with debonair gaiety, to indicate to us all that it was a happy drunk she was on, with no tone of her vicious ones.

But how precariously near we had come to an outbreak of war in our own little center of the world. We have peace, a blessed peace, but we cannot say it is a peace with worldly justice. No, according to justice, Miss L should have been cast on this occasion into outer darkness. She was the aggressor. But we were appeasers. If she had been cast out, then she would have ended up in a police station and returned to us with black eyes and bruised face (that had happened before). By our accepting with meekness her effrontery, her insults, and the nuisance of her behavior, we shortened our time of visitation, and our mercy met with her gratitude in her sober return to her senses, and there are longer and longer intervals in her drinking periods.

"And the point of that is," Peter would say, "people learn the art of human contacts by living in a House of Hospitality. And workers should be scholars and scholars workers." As he pointed out in one of his essays:

Scholars and Bourgeois

The scholar has told the bourgeois that
a worker is a man for all of that.

But the bourgeois has told the scholar
that a worker is a commodity for all of that.
Because the scholar has vision
the bourgeois calls him a visionary.
So the bourgeois laughs at the scholar's vision
and the worker is left without vision.
And the worker left by the scholar without vision
talks about liquidating
both the bourgeois and the scholar.
The scholars must tell the worker
what is wrong
with things as they are.
The scholars must tell the workers
how things would be,
if they were as they should be.
The scholars must tell the workers
how a path can be made
from things as they are
to things as they should be.
The scholars must collaborate with the workers
in the making of a path
from things as they are
to things as they should be.
The scholars must become workers
so the workers may become scholars.

* * *

Peter's idea of a valiant woman, as is that of the Church, is the picture of the holy woman portrayed in the thirty-first book of Proverbs:

Who shall find a valiant woman?
Far from the uttermost coasts is the price of her.
The heart of her husband trusteth in her;
And he shall have no need of spoils.

She will do him good and not evil
All the days of her life.
She hath sought wool and flax,
And hath wrought by the counsel of her hands.
She is like the merchant's ship;
She bringeth her bread from afar,
And she has risen in the night, and given a prey
            to her household,
And victuals to her maidens.
She hath considered a field and bought it.
With the fruit of her hand she hath planted a vineyard . . .

This, of course, is the picture of a queen, sung by her son Lemuel, but Peter would apply it to a woman in the slums, to a peasant woman on the land.

The poem depicts Peter's vision of a philosophy of labor, of love and joy in work, a sense of the beauty of work. It clearly emphasizes the sense of personal responsibility, the practice of the works of mercy, the care for others around her, the selflessness of a mother of a household.

In discussing women Peter always gets back to his thesis that people in the cities are cut off from the sources of life by the urban cultural pattern.

All great civilizations, he points out, have been based on a sound agriculture. The cities of the past have been comparatively small, and represent the flowering of the culture of the countryside.

"Woman is matter, man is spirit," Peter said one time, and none of us understood him.

But he was thinking of woman and her nature, which is so close to the sources of life, most completely herself when she is caring for growing things, providing for them, feeding them, clothing them. It is not an empty phrase—"Mother Earth," fecund, warm, rich, constant, and silent.

Meditating on these things, one begins to understand what Peter means when he says, "Woman is matter." Unless she uses her body

*to produce and her hands to serve her young, she is unfulfilled, unde-
veloped, stunted, and thwarted.*

*The valiant woman was strong—she put her hand to strong
things. She bore burdens, she worked late, "she hath risen in the
night," "her lamp shall not be put out." Yet always strong, healthy—
"she hath strengthened her arm, she hath tasted and seen that her
traffic is good."*

*The peculiar lack of balance in our present-day living is epito-
mized for Peter by the fact that the rich, who have earned their
money by factories, value the "handmade."*

*"You too can be rich," cries Peter, "you too can put your hands
to the crafts, furnish homes, weave and spin, bake bread. Then you
will value what you have produced. Then you will put yourself into
it. Then you will have given yourself. Then you will begin to understand the sacramentality of life. You will understand the sacramen-
tal principles, you will begin to see God in all things. You will look
upon what God has made, and find it good. You will look at things
as God looks at them. You will begin to have the mentality of sons
of God, daughters of God."*

* * *

In the final section of this chapter, Dorothy Day reflects on
Peter Maurin's ideas and concludes that at the core of Maurin's
vision are the radical concepts of voluntary poverty and personalism. Since as a personalist he never accepted force as a means
to realize his vision, violence was not in his vocabulary. He
believed in the one-person revolution becoming the two-person
revolution, and so on. He won his victories one at a time, for he
believed that each individual was also a spiritual being connected
to eternity, and his vision of things as they should be occurred in
the fullness of time, not a fragment of it. For him there was no
four- or five-year plan. Without the demand of time he felt no
need to persuade or force his point of view, a strange position for
a radical and one that makes him easy to dismiss. His idea would
not be realized in a great explosion in the pattern of human his-

tory. It would settle itself into the rhythm of time. His was a universal revolution for which the person, not the movement, was preeminent. If there truly were a God (and he believed there was) all humanity would evolve to a point where the infinite values of community would become one with the finite.

Voluntary poverty was the radical manifestation of his program. His was not the degrading poverty of the abandoned and downtrodden, but rather the spiritually enriching poverty that can say no to the rush for pleasure in things. His idea of poverty was one that saw things for their utility, not the joy of their possession. It was a poverty that proposed living in a manner that all might live equally well. Dorothy Day's reflections on Maurin clarify these points.

Many a time Peter made what he called "points," but I did not get the idea for months. He built up a program of action, his listeners conceded the necessity for working out such a program, and then he expected them to guide their lives thereby, readjusting themselves to these news ideas that he presented. If he failed to influence others as he had hoped, he shrugged his shoulders and went on propounding social theories. He was content to wait until circumstances arrived which would be more favorable to the presentation of his ideas. Whether he considered that those in the Catholic Worker movement had made vague beginnings in his three-point program, I do not know. Certainly he has, through the circulation of The Catholic Worker, *which is now sixty thousand readers, found for himself many readers and many listeners.*

He had invitations to speak at colleges, seminaries, and groups throughout the country. Through the Houses of Hospitality which have been established he has built up groups for round-table discussion. Through the farming communes he has directed attention to fundamental economic ideas.

To him, there was a synthesis to all his ideas. They fit together. And as blueprints for a new world they are unsurpassed. But when it came to working them out, given the human material, the lack of equipment, the vagaries of human nature, there was the rub! Do they work? Does Christianity work? If it fails it is glorious in its failure, the failure of the cross.

I do know this, that when people come into contact with Peter Maurin, they change, they awaken, they begin to see, things become as new, they look at life in the light of the Gospels. They admit the truth he possesses and lives by, and though they themselves fail to go the whole way, their faces are turned at least toward the light. And Peter was patient. Looking at things as he did in the light of history, taking the long view, he was content to play his part, to live by his principles and wait. As Pascal said, "It is not ours to see the triumph of the truth but to fight in its behalf."

I have always thought of Peter as an Apostle to the world. In the essays printed in The Catholic Worker, many of them contain an outline of history, a criticism of history, an outline of simple solutions. They have to do with the world, this life which we know and love, with the needs of our bodies for food, clothing, and shelter. His philosophy, his sociology, his economics, have a truly religious foundation. There is a synthesis in his instructions to us all. "Cult, Culture, Cultivation" is not just a catchy phrase under which he listed his quotations. Peter has emphasized most steadily that famous quote of Chesterton, "Christianity has not failed—it has been found difficult and left untried."

Father [Paul Hanley] Furfey of Catholic University in his recent book, The History of Social Thought, brings out in his first chapter how long the history of the human race is. Richarz, he says, has summarized the evidence which proves that thirty thousand years is the absolute minimum, and then goes on to talk about early human remains of the Pleistocene period, which began from three hundred thousand to a million years ago, with the weight of opinion inclining more and more to the larger figure. By the side of these figures, the 1942 years of Christianity seem relatively an instant in the history of the world.

With this fresh point of view, Peter did not find it extraordinary to expect people to try to begin now to put into practice some of the social ideas, not only of the New Testament, but of the Old. Unless we try to put these ideas into practice we are guilty of secularism.

*Unless we are trying to put the social ideas of the Gospel into prac-
tice, we are not showing our love for our neighbor. And as St. John
wrote, "How can we love God whom we have not seen, unless we
love our brother whom we do see." Unless we are putting these social
ideas into practice, recognizing the correlation of soul and body, we
are using religion as an insurance policy, as a prop, as a comfort in
affliction, and not only is religion then truly an opiate of the people,
but we are like men who "beholding our face in the glass, go away,
not mindful of what manner of men we are."*

*Peter did not talk subjectively about religion. He brought to us
quotations and books and ideas that, by stimulating the mind to
know, would encourage the heart to love. Three quotations from the
first letter of St. John epitomize Peter's religious attitude for me.*

*"No man hath seen God at any time. If we love one another,
God abideth in us; and His charity is perfected in us. . . ."*

*"If any man say: 'I love God,' and hateth his brother; he is a
liar. For he that loveth not his brother whom he seeth, how can he
love God whom he seeth not? . . ."*

*"He that hath the substance of this world and shall see his
brother in need and shall shut up his heart from him; how doth the
charity of God abide in him?"*

*And there is that sentence of St. James, "If a brother or sister be
naked and want daily food, and one of you say to them, 'Go in peace,
be ye warmed and filled,' yet give them not those things that are necessary for the body, what shall it profit?"*

*And of course to sum it all up, there are those never-to-be-
forgotten words of our Lord, "Inasmuch as ye have done it unto the
least of these My brethren, ye have done it unto Me."*

*It is the above quotations that point the reason for Peter's pre-
occupation with the material details of this world, with the social
order, with the need for rebuilding, as he says, "within the shell of
the old, with a philosophy which is so old that it looks like new."*

*And this preoccupation of his with business, with economics,
with agriculture, with labor, with capital, with credit unions,
maternity guilds, with cooperatives, his unceasing emphasis on the
fact that these are the vital concerns of religion have led people to*

think of him as a materialist. "Laying too much emphasis on the material!" they say piously, and return to their prayers. "After all, we must use our spiritual weapons, we must devote ourselves to religious service and these things will be added unto us." And withdrawing themselves, "keeping themselves unspotted from the world," they again are guilty of secularism, of using religion as an opiate.

Peter talked about asceticism as a neglected study. Being the soul of delicacy, he did not go so far as our Benedictine friend, Fr. Joseph, who said that dogmatic theology taught people to get into Heaven with scorched behinds. When Peter talked about asceticism it was as matter-of-factly, as the word implies, "an exercise" of one's religion. To him, religion and asceticism go together. It is inconceivable for instance that one can truly be "religious" and not embrace voluntary poverty.

And it is this emphasis on voluntary poverty that has led to much criticism and antagonism toward the movement, even while it has called forth the most attention and attracted the most admiration. Unfortunately, the admiration has come from those who contemplate from afar, and the criticism from those close to us has much justice in it.

On account of the emphasis placed upon poverty in the past which led to heresies (an overemphasis of one aspect of the truth, to the expense of others) probably not enough has been written about poverty in the present, especially here in the United States, when modern plumbing seems to epitomize culture and civilization.

When Jesus gathered his disciples and the multitude around him to preach the Sermon on the Mount, he was not just addressing the disciples when he said, "Ye are the salt of the earth." He was addressing the poor. The rest of his discourse was meant for them, the Beatitudes were for them, so he meant also to call them the salt of the earth. The poor are the salt of the earth; the truly poor, the poor in spirit.

What a mysterious thing poverty is. To the religious-minded, it has had an enormous attraction through the ages. To simplify one's life, to cut out the superfluous, to go against the sensual inclinations *of one's own nature—Christian and non-Christian alike, have emphasized these teachings.*

There is William James's panegyric on poverty:

> *When we gravely ask ourselves whether this wholesale organization of irrationality and crime (war) be our only bulwark against effeminacy, we stand aghast at the thought, and think more kindly of ascetic religion. One hears of the mechanical equivalent of heat. What we need to discover in the social realm is the moral equivalent of war; something heroic that will speak to men as universally as war does, and yet be as compatible with their spiritual selves as war has proved to be incompatible.*

> *I have often thought that in the old monkish poverty-worship, in spite of the pedantry which infested it, there might be something like that moral equivalent of war which we are seeking. May not voluntarily accepted poverty be the strenuous life without the need of crushing weaker peoples? Poverty indeed is the strenuous life without brass bands or uniforms or hysteric popular applause or lies or circumlocutions; and when one sees the way in which wealth-giving enters as an ideal into the very bone and marrow of our generation, one wonders whether a revival of the belief that poverty is a worthy religious vocation may not be the transformation of military courage and the spiritual reform which our time stands as most in need of.*

> *Among us English-speaking people especially do the praises of poverty need once more to be boldly sung. We have grown literally afraid to be poor. We despise anyone who elects to be poor in order to simplify and save his inner life. If he does not join the general scramble and pant with the moneymaking street, we deem him spiritless and lacking in ambition. We have lost the power even of imagining what the ancient idealization of poverty could have meant: the liberation from material attachments, the unbridled soul, the manlier indifference, the paying our way by what*

we are to do and not what we have, the right to fling away our life at any moment irresponsibly—the more athletic trim, in short, the moral fighting shape. When we of the so-called better classes are scared as men were never scared in history at material ugliness and hardship; when we put off marriage until our house can be artistic, and quake at the thought of having a child without a bank account and doomed to manual labor, it is time for thinking men to protest against so unmanly and irreligious a state of opinion. It is true that so far as wealth gives time for ideal ends and exercise to ideal energies, wealth is better than poverty and ought to be chosen.

But wealth does this in only a portion of the actual cases. Elsewhere the desire to gain wealth and fear to lose it are our chief breeders of cowardice and propagators of corruption. There are thousands of conjunctures in which a wealth-bound man must be a slave, whilst a man for whom poverty has no terrors becomes a free man. Think of the strength which personal indifference to poverty would give us if we were devoted to unpopular causes. We need no longer hold our tongues or fear to vote the revolutionary or reform ticket. Our stocks might fall, our hopes of promotion vanish, our salaries stop, our club doors close in our face; yet while we lived we would imperturbably bear witness to the spirit, and our example would help us to set free our generation. The cause would need its funds, but we its servants would be potent in proportion as we personally were contented with our poverty.

I recommend this matter to your serious pondering, for it is certain that the prevalent fear of poverty among the educated classes is the worst moral disease from which our civilization suffers.

One of our Italian neighbors has an extravagant fear of poverty. When we took over one of the apartments in the front building there were so many locks and bars and bolts that one would have thought there was a vendetta in the neighborhood.

I looked at those bolts and bars. The family was not afraid of public opinion; it was the strongest family in the neighborhood. They were not afraid of the law; the matriarch of the family sold liquor in her kitchen, without a license, as many of the families did, and other members had gotten into trouble with the law. They were not afraid of God himself, since none of them went to church. They were afraid of neither God nor man, but they were afraid of losing their money. That was the greatest terror life had to offer.

There is St. Francis—the heart leaps at the thought of him, loved by Catholic and non-Catholic. Once a priest pointed to a statue of St. Francis and said sadly, "There is the last Franciscan."

Bernanos in his Diary of a Country Priest *understood poverty, as did Léon Bloy, who wrote* The Woman Who Was Poor.

Poverty is hard to understand. It is an inexhaustible mine of wisdom. "Those who are in honor are without understanding," the Psalmist said. Christ did not try to rescue people from their poverty. He came to preach the gospel. When he fed the multitude—and there are two stories of such miracles in the Gospel—the people must have wanted him to go on feeding them. But he fed them once, taking compassion on them so that they did not go away hungry. It must have been a suffering all though his life not to feed people in their poverty. It was one of the temptations of the devil, who said to him, "Turn these stones into bread." It would have been so easy for him to feed them, to relieve their hunger. He must have seen many hungry, many suffering, and many begging. Remembering this, and living in poverty ourselves, is the only way we can endure life, which is so filled with suffering these days. Yet by poverty we do not mean destitution. Henri Daniel-Rops in The Poor and Ourselves *makes a distinction between poverty and destitution.*

To us, poverty has been a mine of wealth and of wisdom, a means to an end. And Peter has among us all most exemplified the man who was poor.

6

Clarification of Thought

༄

A Leader
is a fellow
who refuses to be crazy
the way everybody else is crazy
and tries to be crazy
in his own crazy way.
    —Peter Maurin

I picked up a biography of Stalin the other day and there was a description of the man and his room, his offices. That is the way I should write about Peter. I should give more of his background. He is short and broad, strongly built, with heavy shoulders and strong arms that are used to pick and shovel. He wears workers' shoes that he buys in the Bowery for three dollars. They are never shined. He wears heavy underwear and it is only at our insistence that he keeps several suits so that he can change. Upon encountering a brother who was cold and asking for help, he would always give away his extra suit, and then with commendable prudence would not change until we found him another one. His other suit had been given him by a friend or reader of the paper and was very baggy in the knees. He washed out the collar and cuffs of his blue work shirt, dried it overnight, and put it on again unironed.

He was a good-looking man, with a broad, full forehead, friendly, warm eyes, straight nose, and pleasant mouth. He laughed delightfully at his own jokes and rejoiced in applause, becoming intensely stimulated at what he took to be a rejoicing understanding of his ideas. That it was sometimes himself that people rejoiced over never entered his head.

We still use the kind of hotel Peter first lived in as an annex to our House of Hospitality on Mott Street. There is just such a hotel on the corner of Hester and the Bowery where we put up many friends who come to stay with us during the summer or during holiday times in winter, when our House of Hospitality is crowded, or when we do not think them quite up to the rigors of cold rooms in winter and vermin in the summer.

Visitors always arrive unexpectedly with us, and unfortunately those amongst us who are most hospitable are often most oblivious to elemental comfort. Those who have not a proper understanding of the work are apt to confuse our basic principles. For instance instead of treating each guest of noble or ill fame that comes to us as Christ himself, we are apt to treat him as a beggar is normally treated. It is so hard to provide food for our daily quota of five hundred, more or less, that soap, insecticides, sheets, and towels are often lacking and have to be purchased on arrival of the visitor. Hence, we often fall back on the "Union," a typical man's lodging on the Bowery which is warm and clean, with hot showers and lockers for one's clothes, the rooms consisting of little cells separated by thin partitions, the top covered with chicken wire to keep an enterprising neighbor from "hooking" one's shoes. Priests, seminarians, and college students coming to call upon us during vacations have often enjoyed the hospitality of the Union. "Clean as a Carthusian monastery, but not as quiet," one priest commented.

Living in such a hotel whenever he came to New York, Peter enjoyed comparative comfort, and as for quiet, he could find that walking the crowded streets. He walked slowly with his hands behind his back. His pockets were always big enough to carry the books and papers he needed. When he traveled with a suitcase it usually contained books, and he checked it at a bus station when he arrived at his destination, and took it out at need. (He often slept in bus stations.)

Marquette University Archives

It was the first winter of the work that Peter moved into the House of Hospitality for good. Not that he had anything to move but the clothes on his back and the books in his pocket. Though he cannot be so comfortable surrounded by so many noisy people, I am sure he enjoys the family atmosphere of the House of Hospitality. For a long, crowded period he shared a room with three others, and his bed and table stood in one rear room, with a lamp over his bed so that he could read at night. He enjoyed discussions that lasted until two or three in the morning and never considered the time wasted in talk "for the clarification of thought."

Perhaps there is too much small talk, too much hanging around, too many young people wisecracking, too much staying up late, but that is unavoidable in a movement that attracts so many. As for the kind of talk one got from Peter—the kind of talk that goes on in unraveling the problems as to human relations, "the art of human contacts," Peter called it—that is necessary and there will never be an end of it.

There is a story of St. Paul talking in the twentieth chapter of Acts. According to the story, Paul talked for so long into the night that a young man sitting on a window sill went to sleep and fell three stories to the ground. The disciples ran down to him, and apparently Paul restored his life and then went back upstairs to continue his discussion. It is like this at the Catholic Worker house. "There can be no revolution without a theory of revolution," Peter quotes Lenin. And Peter's long talks evolved and clarified the theory of his Green Revolution.

He himself slept until ten and then fasted until midday mass at St. Andrew's Church down on Duane Street, near City Hall, about a four-block walk from the house.

For a long time he had the first floor rear room all to himself in the back of the library. It was not the safest place to put him as he was quite apt to give all the books away, but it was a delight for him to be among the books. They were probably his one "attachment," but he was so lavish in giving them away.

Peter's room was small and square, with bed, desk, file cabinet, table and chair. Everything was neat and everything was dusty. He never noticed dust or dirt, but he did like to have everything in its place. Peter's room was in the rear building on the next street, which rises five stories high. There is never any sun or daylight in this room. It is truly a dungeon. But then every rear room in the house is the same, and the front rooms, facing another five-story building twenty feet away, get daylight on bright days but sunlight only for a brief hour or so during the day. We live by artificial light. These rear buildings used to be fronted by a long garden, but as the city grew up another building rose in front, leaving only a square courtyard between. It is in this courtyard that two or three hundred men gather before lunch and dinner, and always there are men mending their shoes or just sleeping against the fence. The two windows in the library, which we also considered Peter's room, face on this scene. No wonder our neighbors, living in just such two- or four-room apartments, spend a good part of their lives on the street, running from one patch of sun to another.

When I think of Peter and his "easy conversations" I think of the apostles coming together on the island of Cyprus—Timothy and Paul, perhaps it was, "and they conversed for a year."

I think too of St. Catherine of Siena and how she used to talk. There is a story told of her that she could talk for twelve hours at a stretch, and when the listener, whether he was priest or bishop, fell asleep under the barrage, she used to wake him up and insist upon his continuing to listen.

Of course, one gets tired of talk as one gets tired of cities and longs for the silence of the desert. One of our favorite stories is that of the three monks who withdrew to the desert to pray. A year passed by and one of them said, "The silence is wonderful here." Another year passed by and the second monk said, "Indeed, yes." Another year passed by and the third monk said, "I think I'm going to go where I can have some peace and quiet."

Among the authentic sayings of the Holy Fathers there is this: "An old man said, 'One man is thought to be silent, and yet his heart judges and condemns others, and the man who acts thus speaks continually; another man speaks from morning till evening and yet keeps silence, that is to say he speaks nothing which is not helpful.'"

Across the hall from this two-room suite there is running water and a toilet, which has been partitioned off from the room. The library has a fireplace, yet because of doors and windows that never fit, and a hall door that is open and shut all day by the hundreds who come to lunch and supper, there are constant drafts. One can heat the place with an oil stove, but then the feet are apt to be cold and the oil stoves are smelly. At least the kind we have are. In the long run one is safer with the open fireplace. There is always driftwood in the rivers, and boxes discarded from the small factories and groceries round about us. One has to compete with all the small boys in the neighborhood for the wood, but our need is great too. At the present, the youngest member of our community is two years of age and the oldest is eighty-five, so heat during a cold winter is a problem.

Ade Bethune, Dorothy Day, Dorothy Weston,
philosopher Jacques Maritain, and Peter Maurin, c. 1934.

One noon I met Peter down at St. Andrew's Church, and we
walked along the Bowery to the Eclipse restaurant, where he usually
had his breakfast. The Eclipse is a large, square, unattractive store,
larger than the usual coffee shop, with the walls painted a swampy
green and the lights not very bright. This is probably a good thing,
because wherever one looks, all is dirt and neglect.

Floors are dirty and covered with sawdust. Cockroaches chase
each other in all directions. I don't mean that they are thick, but
wherever you look, between the piles of bread, on the counter, under
the edges of the tables, on the floor at your feet, on the wall where
you hang your coat you always see a scurrying insect. It is the same
in our own Houses of Hospitality.

Not that this condition is known only to those on the Bowery.
One of our friends, a priest at a Benedictine priory, in order to com-
fort us when we were having coffee in our kitchen at Saint Joseph's
House, told us about the cockroaches in their kitchen where they have

a good deal of help. "Only the other night," he said, "I had missed supper and was looking for a snack in the ice box and there were so many cockroaches swarming over the box I was afraid to open the door for fear of letting them in. So I went to bed without anything to eat."

And last week I spoke in the hall of a Catholic institution where huge water bugs scurried this way and that around the floor at my feet. The priest who sat next to me killed one, but after we saw three or four others we didn't bother.

I certainly don't think the poor ever get used to cockroaches, bed-bugs, body lice, fleas, and similar vermin that go with poverty. They merely endure them, sometimes with patience, sometimes with a cor-roding bitterness that the comfortable and pious stigmatize as envy. Someone asked Peter once why God had created bedbugs, and he said, "For practicing our patience, probably."

After creating this vivid scene of the life of the poor on the Lower East Side, Day brings readers into the scene by having them sit down with Peter and her in a local restaurant.

The restaurant was filled with small tables, all of them crowded. Peter and I sat down with two Negroes. These left during the course of our conversation and two sailors, heavily tattooed, took their places. They might have been Scandinavian, Finnish, Russian—it's hard to tell the nationality of these men. On the walls were half a dozen cracked mirrors, some of them broken completely in half, and on the fragments painted with chalk, food was advertised.

Pig ears, spaghetti, bread and tea, 15 cents

Fried mush, one egg, coffee, 15 cents

Peter ordered lamb stew, which came at once, a huge bowl of it with three slices of bread and a very large mug of coffee, all for 20 cents.

It seemed to me that at every table around, everyone was eating the same lamb stew, and when I ordered fried mush with an egg, the waiter shook his head uncomprehendingly and said, "Lamb stew." So I ordered it too. It was hot and good. There were a few pieces of potato and carrot, plenty of meat, and plenty of grease. Over on the counter there were desserts, and here they served not one baked apple, but three. Evidently they cater to robust appetites.

We were looking at the daily paper, as we went in, containing a story of a mine strike; also an account of a CIO convention. We began talking of labor leaders and Peter said: "Murray seems to be a religious man. John Lewis is a Welshman and the Welsh are very much akin to the Bretons. They are often mystics but mysticism may go in the wrong direction. From God-centered, they may become man-centered. Murray is a Catholic. They say he prays. I don't know about Lewis. I hear he has no religion. There may be the will to power. His mysticism may take that form, but I don't know. Murray has made an important analysis of unemployment. People fail to realize the importance of intelligent analysis of a situation before anything else can be done about it."

Since Peter was hungry he talked more or less in fragments so we had no time on this occasion to talk in detail about the labor situation. I mentioned that we had an engagement for next Monday with Helene Isvolsky, the author of Soviet Man Now, *and other books on Russia, which I read with much interest. Also she has had articles in* Commonweal. *Her father, Peter said, "was a Russian diplomat and formulated the foreign policies in the time of the czar."*

Peter went on eating his lamb stew with great appetite. He had been traveling all night, coming from Philadelphia, where the Catechetical Congress had been going on the last few days. I had asked him to go down there because many bishops were very interested in Peter's ideas. Bishop Eustace of Camden, Bishop O'Hara of Kansas City, who is head of the conference, Bishop Boyle of Pittsburgh, Bishop Armstrong of Sacramento—I don't know how many he saw. In a huge congress of this kind, I don't imagine there was much chance to talk.

Peter did not look in the least bit tired, but of course, he looked rather dirty, traveling as he had done, jumping from New York to Boston then back to Philadelphia, and then back home again. His shirt was wilted, and his suit crushed and unpressed. It hadn't been cleaned for a long time because he had no other suit.

As Peter finished up the last crumbs of his bread and the last drops of stew, he looked around him and called attention to the type of workers. "Not many loafers here," he said. "Contractors come down here to the Bowery and get these men for railroad jobs or contracting jobs. Sometimes there is intelligent conversation with intelligent criticism. I worked with these gangs going out of Chicago once. They didn't give us our pay. Only paper, which we were supposed to cash when we got back to Chicago. We had to take a boxcar back, and we were arrested for that and thrown in jail. We had to walk a good part of the day, and we took corn from the fields and ate it raw."

I thought of Christ and his disciples, as he said this.

"I was with a Finn from [Helsinki]. As soon as he got to Chicago he drank up all his money. They don't get much, of course, and many of them drink."

"How did you make out at the Socialist meeting at Boston?" I asked.

"All right," said Peter. "The other speaker tried to bring them a philosophy of private property from the pope's encyclicals. I gave him the philosophy, or the essence of it. Of course, they would only give me twenty minutes so I had to keep it short."

"Do you remember which essays you gave?" I asked.

"I only took a few. Of course I had to select here and there to give the essence. I started with the idea of 'Folk Schools.' Then 'Logical and Practical,' 'Real Man,' 'Better and Better Off,' 'Big Shots and Little Shots,' 'Two of a Kind,' and 'Tug of War.'"

These are the titles of some of what Dorothy Day called Maurin's Easy Essays. He wrote them in blank verse. They summarized his ideas and they were published a few at a time in the monthly paper.

Marjorie Crowe had joined us while we ate and had taken down Peter's remarks in shorthand, so I give them here to convey their flavor, even with his naïve delight in his ideas, which were beginning to be heard.

"I told them I am the son of a peasant who could neither read nor write, so I am precapitalistic. Yes I am precapitalistic and I don't like capitalism and I don't like socialism, which is the child of capi-

talism: That is father and son. I don't like the father and I don't like the son."

"How many were there at the meeting?"

"Not many. They didn't advertise it."

"That's good. We don't like advertising."

"I told them about the fallacy of saving and the wisdom of giving—I left them with a number of things to think about. 'The First Christians,' 'Self-Organization,' 'On the Farming Commune,' 'Firing the Boss.' 'The Land of the Refugee,' 'Free Guest Houses,' 'Rural Centers in Ireland,' 'The Irish Scholars' [more Easy Essay titles] and I told them they don't have to keep up with the Irish politicians. They can keep up with the Irish scholars and go in for Irish communism."

"That's a good, positive program for Boston," I observed.

"I told them of the communism that was brought by the Jesuits to the Indians in Paraguay, and by the Franciscans to the Indians of Texas, Arizona, New Mexico, and California. A fellow who was interested said, 'How is it that they got out of Paraguay?' And I was telling him that the Indians in Paraguay don't like the white people. They were keeping away from the Jesuits because they were white, because the whites robbed them and made slaves of them. And so the Jesuits formed there a communal life and gave guns and told them to shoot whites when whites tried to force them into slavery. So friends of the white people were complaining to the bishops in Europe against the Jesuits exciting the Indians; and the pope, who was a Franciscan, suppressed the Jesuits because they had given arms. There was an old man from Austria there at the meeting who knew all about it, who even knew the name of the pope.

"Then I gave them a philosophy of history and that interested them. They don't know these things. That gives them a light. Glass, a socialist at the meeting, called us Christian communists—but he was trying to figure out the encyclicals on the social order. These encyclicals, I told him, were trying to make an acquisitive society functional. We consider this society a product of capitalism, and we are trying to go back to a functional society; one that we had once, before it decayed *into acquisitiveness. The encyclicals try to convert an acquisitive society into a functional society. We personally renounce the acquisitive society altogether. It is a question of techniques.*

"The original guilds had the idea. There is a pamphlet, 'The Sound Old Guilds.' Glass had a better conception of guilds than most people. There were no guilds in rural districts. What they had was an ideology: the ideology of the gospel.

"If the capitalists are eager for change, they would start associations of Catholic employers. They don't. They just talk about it. They would have the cooperation of the ACTU, which fosters changing an acquisitive society into a functional one."

Maurin is not only criticizing capitalists, but also the members of the ACTU who, according to Maurin, naively believed they could reach a meaningful compromise with capitalism. But Maurin believed that capitalists payed lip service to such groups without taking them seriously. The ACTU—the Association of Catholic Trade Unionists—grew out of the Catholic Worker movement in the thirties. Founded by John Cort, the movement attempted to present the Catholic view of labor to the emerging industrial labor movement. They sponsored labor schools and assisted in organizing a number of important labor struggles of the mid-1930s. According to Dorothy Day, their aim was "to assist the worker to organize and to enlighten Catholics in existing trade unions . . . they set out at once to oppose the Communist and the gangster elements in the longshoreman and other unions." Their endorsement of union activity in essence accepted the industrial capitalist status quo that put them into conflict with Maurin, who saw his program as long-range. His program advocated ownership by the workers of the means of production, the abolition of the assembly line, and a decentralization of factories.[1] Maurin's monologue continued:

"We go back to the simple life. Even Thoreau was talking about it and Gandhi is an admirer of Thoreau. The National Catholic Welfare Conference used to be connected with the Rural Life Conference.

The Catholic Rural Life Conference talks about homesteads. We favor communes. What we foster did exist at one time. We go back.

"It was the same with the House of Hospitality. We had to prove to the bishops it could be done. The bishop of Sacramento says it almost does itself. It is not like people asking for money and saying, 'rely on our judgment.' It is people who give of themselves to the leaders.

"Some will tell me that it is not in the encyclicals. They don't know the encyclicals. The one on St. Francis, for instance. Ours is Franciscan and Benedictine stuff. They have abandoned Franciscanism and so we will show them the way by proving it can be done.

"The idea is now people don't work if they don't get wages. Even the workers become just as acquisitive as the Chambers of Commerce. We know some workers can't take it. Some get drunk. They become intoxicated with spirits. We think if they can become intoxicated with the Spirit they won't care about spirits anymore.

"Father Gillis says things are becoming worse. But when things become worse, people cease to be indifferent. That is the hardest thing to contend with—indifference. People are preoccupied about the problems of this world. About people living in this world. If we were more preoccupied about the next world maybe it would solve the problems of this world, too. People are beginning to pay attention to the priests and the bishops now.

"Gerry was saying the bishops' statement seemed to please nobody. We have to present social teaching in such a way—that is where intelligence wins—that the religious orders would profess those things. But the problem is that the religious orders have become like the professors that don't profess. They say that my ideas, which were their traditional ideas, are not practical. But who is the doubter of practicality? Now they admit the House of Hospitality idea is practical. And my cracks—logic with cracks—are not considered any longer to be wisecracks and they give me a hearing. So I got bishops reading my stuff now.

"When the Abbot of Saint Meinrad was here he asked me, 'Where do you get all those ideas?' I told him I didn't get them—they got me. Now they give me a hearing.

"The secretaries wouldn't listen to me but I have succeeded in getting over their secretaries. Because they think I've got something on the ball. Through carrying out the farming commune program we prove we may be able to bring the Franciscans back to Franciscanism. And if you bring the Franciscans back to Franciscanism you will have the stuff for the Jesuits too, as well as the Benedictines. When the Jesuits and Benedictines and Franciscans get our line of practicality then the Knights of Columbus will get it too. And when the Knights of Columbus get it then the Free Masons will get it, and the Free Masons will be both free and masons. Masons because they will construct. When the ideas get me I got to express them, because people expect that from me."

Not so long ago I asked Stanley Vishnewski to clip every one of Peter's Easy Essays from back issues of the Catholic Worker *and put them in shape so we could classify them. Peter believes in repetition, and many a time he gives us the same essays for the paper, grouped differently with perhaps a few new essays added to make a new point. He likes to use every modern means to drive home new ideas. He uses the soapbox in Columbus Circle, and the group discussions in Union Square. He wanted to make records of his Easy Essays, and it was all I could do to prevent him from making a number of them and playing them over and over again, with a loudspeaker to the bread line grouped in the backyard. The tactic smacked too much of* Brave New World, *only in the Huxley book it was babies who were broadcasted to while they slept. I believe there was some little instrument under their pillows making points to them so they would be conditioned thereby.*

In going over all of Peter's essays and weeding out his duplicated ones, I found that he had written very few on Houses of Hospitality. What he had written he used again and again.

Maurin, as Day noted, wrote little on Houses of Hospitality because it remained at the periphery of his vision. Houses of Hospitality, however, became central to Dorothy Day. Even in this biography of Maurin, her predilections predominate. In the following paragraphs and in the next chapter of this manuscript,

Day wandered away from her subject to explain how she took Maurin's vision of a new economy and new social system based on decentralization of industry and small-scale agriculture and transformed it into a plan to help the urban poor. Her commitment to Maurin's Christian personalism was the glue that bonded the apparently divergent plans. Day was Maurin's best student; she followed his counsel to begin the revolution by simply beginning, by doing what one does best, with the personalist vision as a guide.

Dorothy's energy, her ability to write and publish, and her commitment to a very specific goal overshadowed Maurin's dream. Consequently, those familiar with the Catholic Worker know it as Dorothy Day's movement. And in fact it is. The Catholic Worker is identified with urban charity, labor, and nonviolence. These were Dorothy Day's passions, not Peter Maurin's. Maurin's role is that he inspired Day; he gave theological and philosophic substance to her own inclinations. For this reason she felt compelled to write his biography. But it is no ordinary narrative of a man's life; it is, rather, an explanation of how Day appropriated Maurin's vision for her own purpose. The following paragraphs clearly demonstrate that although it may have been Maurin's philosophy, it was Dorothy Day's energy and commitment to the poor that created the Catholic Worker movement, as it currently exists. In the following pages Day began by explaining Maurin's thought in relation to the Houses of Hospitality. But the narrative departs from Maurin, just as in reality her actions left him and his true vision unrealized.

The basis of his thought on Houses of Hospitality is that Christians should love one another and take care of one another as they did in early Christian days. There should be a guest room, "a Christ room," as the early Fathers called it, in every home: "The coat that hangs in your closet belongs to the poor." There should be hospices as there were in the Middle Ages, connected with every monastery, every big Catholic institution, throughout the country, whether schools, colleges, universities, hospitals, seminaries, or monasteries. As a matter of fact there are many bread lines connected with Catholic institutions, but the need for shelter in this day and age is more imperative than the need of bread, and people are reluctant to shelter the poor, for fear they will have this burden on their backs forever. They are afraid of "pauperizing" the poor. They are afraid of contributing to their delinquency. They want to move them along, to take care of the greatest number in the shortest possible time, to have something to show for their efforts.

"How long do you let your people stay?" is one of the questions asked. Sometimes the poor are called "cases" or "clients." One social worker wanted to know what our "caseload" was. And our answer is, "We let them stay forever. They live with us, they die with us, and we give them a Christian burial. We pray for them after they are dead. Once they are taken in, they become members of the family. Or rather they were always members of our family. They are our brothers and sisters in Christ."

To make such a statement to public authority is to run the risk of being committed to a psychiatric ward.

On one occasion I was visiting that ward at Bellevue Hospital in order to get one of our women out. She had been attacked on the street, on her way home one evening, and when she complained hysterically to a policeman, she was committed to the psychiatric ward. The police admitted evidences of such an attack; nevertheless, she found herself in this mental ward for examination and was accused of having a persecution complex.

"What interest is it of yours?" the doctor asked me. "She is not a relative. You have no responsibility in the matter. I should think you'd be glad the state is taking care of her."

But we had known her for some years. We felt capable of taking care of her until she was capable of taking care of herself. We assured him of this and told him moreover that she was our sister according to Christian teaching.

The doctor looked at me sadly. "Do you know that religious mania is the most dangerous kind?"

One of the women in the house complained to the health department about the kitchen. She did not like the food that was being served. For a long time after that we were receiving visits from the health department. "We are willing to look upon your people in the house as members of a family," they finally conceded, "but we must look upon the bread line as the public." And for that year they forced us to take out a license "to run a restaurant."

In one diocese I asked for a house owned by the church, to use for a hospice, and the chancellor refused, saying that they would run into difficulties with the health department, the fire department, etc.

It is true that regulations designed for the good of the public are used again and again as a club over the head of institutions. Once a Mother Superior of an order sent us scores of beds because they did not conform to state regulations. In many cases the institutions have taken aid from the state, so the state has stepped in and imposed its regulations, many of them quite senseless.

Of course, as Pope Pius XI has pointed out, in many times of crisis the state must intervene to take care of the common good. In times of depression, in times of national catastrophe, the state has the duty to take care of the homeless, the poverty-stricken. But even in those times, it is to be understood that all Christians, all men of good will, must do their share first in order to relieve the state of much of the burden. It is only after we have used all our own resources that we should call upon the state. It is only when our insurance, our bank savings, our own families, our own Church can no longer care for us that we should look to the state.

But natural pride, a "praiseworthy pride" the majority would say, makes it preferable to receive from the impersonal state. "We have it coming to us. We pay taxes. It is our right." Again, it is justice people demand, not charity. "Away with it, crucify it," people say. "Away with charity, we will have none of it." We don't want to be the least of these, Christ's children. We do not want to share his poverty. "He had no place to lay his head. The birds of the air have their nests and the fox his hole, but the Son of Man has no place to lay his head." "We are not of his company. We do not know the man." We deny him once, twice, thrice, and we have got the habit and go on denying him.

Peter addressing a retreat at the Easton Catholic Worker Farm, 1940.

What a strange point of view, the Christian! What an upside-down point of view. What an unusual point of view. But it is the supernatural point of view. To rejoice in tribulation, to love your enemy, to turn the other cheek—is it natural? "No," *is the response,* "and it is not manly, and surely Christ did not mean all that, and we are not to take him literally. No, if anyone insults me, I'll let him have it. If anyone spits at me, I'll knock him down. If anyone encroaches on my rights, I will stick up for them. After all, it is my family, my home, my country. You cannot take these things literally. This is the time for more militant virtues."

Recently, one of our friends visiting us was irked by our statements in the Catholic Worker on Caesarism and personalism. He kept referring to Uncle Sam all during the dinner. There was talk of farming communities, and jobs and land distribution after the war, yet he kept saying staunchly, "Uncle Sam will take care of it." When the Negro question came up, he would say again, "Uncle Sam will take care of it," as though he were saying, "It is as God wills, it is in God's hands."

And this attitude has been growing for some time now, so steadily and imperceptibly, that the state has taken over one function after another, in addition to the function of charity. "We have no king but Caesar." Yes, it is true that the poor are fed at Catholic institutions. But they are not sheltered. There are no Christ rooms in our houses.

And people have their objections: "But we might be murdered in our beds."

The thing to do then is take in half a dozen people. Take in a family. There is safety in numbers; they will help take care of each other.

"But we haven't the means."

God would not send the poor to you and not provide the means. If you show enough faith by seeing Christ in those who come to you, in receiving the Holy Family when there is no room at the inn, then God will reward that faith. We have proved this over and over again in our Houses of Hospitality throughout the country. And God has shown us over and over through the ages. Oh, if we would only nourish the mustard seed of faith in our breasts, how it would grow into a great and lovely tree to shelter us.

"But we must consider the family."

We concede that objection. A husband must recognize his wife's limitations, and the wife her husband's. To each perhaps is not given the same measure of faith. And they are one flesh. But the ideal marriage would be that in which each vied with the other in charity.

"But we haven't enough for ourselves. Our houses are not large enough."

The second statement is true perhaps, but big houses are falling into decay. People don't want them anymore. And they want modern conveniences, which the big houses do not possess. But we could have done without so many things in order to help our brothers—car, radios, even the overheating of our houses.

"But to love your brother is not so easy," many protest.

There is that scene between Father Zossima and the widow in The Brothers Karamazov. The widow likes to dream of loving the poor, and the old monk tells her, "Love in action is a harsh and dreadful thing compared to love in dreams." How easy it is to take care of the deserving poor. How hard it is to take in as a member of your family those who repay you with scorn and contempt, by quarreling and bickering, by contention and murmuring, who try to kill body and soul in their depravity, or those around them, or those dear to you.

Yes, it is no easy thing to ask. It is no light burden to place on others, this burden of Christianity. But we are not the ones who place this burden on others. Christ, who said, "Take up your cross and follow me," placed it there, and that cross is very often our brother.

The greatest temptation Christ had to suffer in the agony in the Garden of Gethsemane, according to Thomas Aquinas, was not to love his fellows anymore.

That is a fearful thought and brings closer to us than ever Christ's humanity. "Hell is not to love anymore," Bernanos wrote in his Diary of a Country Priest.

It is easy to love one's friends, those who are naturally lovable, those from whom we receive delights of soul or body. But "love in action is a harsh and dreadful thing compared to love in dreams." We have repeated it over and over. It is no new statement on our part, no new attitude.

But several of our friends, in criticizing the theological tone of The Catholic Worker paper recently criticized our attitude toward the poor. "You must be careful not to use the poor as stepping stones into heaven," they warn.

Yes, we understand the necessity of being Christ-centered, not self-centered, not thinking in terms of our own welfare, eternal or temporal. And it is because we can only show our love for God by our love for the poor (because how can we love God whom we have not seen, if we do not love our neighbor whom we do see?) that we talk so much of this love.

We think in terms of the Mystical Body of Christ. We are all members, one of another, and Christ is our head. We share in each other's sins just as we share in each other's virtues. When the health of one member suffers, the health of the whole body is lowered. An injury to one is an injury to all. War, whether it is international or class war, and even when it is enmity between brothers, is a rending of the Mystical Body of Christ.

When my brother sins, it is my sin. "Who will deliver me from the body of this death?" I feel in my own body the sins I see around me. "Those things which I would do, I do not, and what I would, I do not do."

And our Houses of Hospitality, which Peter Maurin inspired, are battlegrounds where gigantic forces are at war with one another, forces of good and evil, and we war not against flesh and blood but against principalities and powers.

It is hard to realize these things, hard to control the motions of the heart. Love is not a sentimental thing, light, airy, romantic, and joyous. It is a matter of the will. "Love in action is a harsh and dreadful thing compared to love in dreams."

7

Houses of Hospitality

༫

The Sermon on the Mount
will be called practical
when Christians make up their mind
to practice it.

—Peter Maurin

Was this what Peter intended? So I often ask myself, as I go around visiting Houses through the country. They are all so different, reflecting the personalities of those who run them.

There is what Peter wrote on the subject, and then there is what is being done. Take the Baltimore house for instance. It is closed now, but I like to think of the Baltimore house, how it started, and how it ran, and how it closed.

Sometimes there is an element of criticism in my thought that the Catholic charities or the chancery office did not prevent the closing. But no, they could do nothing, after all. It deserved to be closed. It was a disgrace. It was folly. It was inefficiently run. There was no order, no justice. And what kind of charity is it when the good suffer for the wicked, when the whole place is wrecked because of an exaggerated idea of brotherly love? After all, we must have some regard for the common good. We must recognize that we are not saints, and that it's no use trying to use tactics of saints.

Catholic Worker breadline.

That is the way most of us argue. It's a shame, though, that the Catholic charities did not take over the old seminary that was empty and use it for the homeless transients, not to speak of the local poor who creep out of the holes and corners of the city like bugs from under a rock just as soon as a bread line starts.

I like to think of that house in Baltimore and I like to think of the boys in charge. It gives me courage, it gives me joy, because they were always rejoicing in tribulation. The worse things were, the calmer and more tranquil they seemed to be. The house held almost two hundred, if half of them were sleeping on the floor. There were beds for only ninety, and the toilet facilities were not too efficient. There were three toilets, and no showers that worked. The men could only wash in the sinks, and they could not clean their clothes or really bathe. Maybe there are public showers in Baltimore, but I do not know of any. The poor get too discouraged to wash—the destitute poor, I mean. Anyway, the beds were verminous, and so were the boys. No matter how many times they cleaned, the vermin came back. It was like a plague of Egypt.

I used to blame the boys, too, until I got the same plague two summers ago, and it took months to get rid of it. Every now and then I found an isolated one crawling on my suit, my dress, or my underwear. Once, at the beginning of my affliction, I went to a tea at the home of Julia Hernan for Jacques Maritain and some other exiles. George Schuster, president of Hunter College, was there and he remarked on the tranquility of my appearance. And underneath, my nerves were shuddering. We do not need hair shirts around Houses of Hospitality.

In Baltimore Jon got sick and had to go to the hospital with influenza, and when the nuns saw his sad plight they thought it was a disgrace. If he had been a soldier just in from the trenches, they would have greeted him as a hero. But he was participating in the class war, taking the stand of nonviolent resistance, of overcoming evil with good. It's a hard position to see. It is not outstanding or heroic from the worldly point of view. It is only little by little that I discovered all that the boys suffered at the house, in their nonviolent resistance to evil. It is not the kind of thing people write about, and it is certainly not the kind of thing one can publish in a family paper. And above all, it cannot be told from the platform.

Over and over again the windows on the first floor of the house were broken by neighbors until finally the boys boarded them up and gave up trying to replace them. Many times I went down there the last two winters to visit them, and always the works of mercy went on—feeding the hungry, sheltering the harborless, giving drink to the thirsty, clothing the naked, visiting the sick, ransoming the prisoner, and burying the dead. And there were also all the spiritual works of mercy; counseling the doubtful, admonishing sinners, bearing wrongs patiently, enlightening the ignorant, comforting the sorrowful, forgiving injuries, and praying for the living and the dead.

It sounds like a large program, but when it comes down to it, the works of mercy don't look like much. They don't make much of a show, unless of course you are multiplying loaves and fish the way Christ did. I always remember, however, that he did not keep on doing it, and they must have wanted him to. And even after the greatest miracle they kept asking for a sign. It is amazing how dangerous the works of mercy are. The fellows in charge of the Baltimore house landed in court quite a few times. Two of them spent nights in jail. On one occasion Jim Thornton had his head shaved by the police, and when he was released the next day, Smitty, another one *of the four who were doing the work, shaved his own head to keep him company.*

Henri Daniel-Ross's book The Poor and Ourselves *points out that there are those who cannot be reached by indoctrination. By their need, by their hunger and their homelessness, by their illness and slow death, they are set apart in their suffering as though a wall were between them and us. We cannot reach them with the gospel. We cannot talk to them of the sweet love of Christ. But we can perform works of mercy.*

I often think that when people merely read about our work and do not know it, they honor us highly and praise us mightily, and reviews and journals and participants at conferences and conventions speak highly of it. Often I am given the most luxurious guest rooms in convents, and I feel out of place indeed. They do not really know the work, the foolishness of it, how little we accomplish, how stupid and inefficient our efforts are or they would not praise us. They would say, "How wonderful God is that he picks out such fools to exemplify such magnificent ideas." But they are trying to show their respect for the gospel in our poor person, I suppose. In Baltimore the folly of our work, even the scandal of it, is revealed in all its intensity.

One of the boys from the Baltimore house who is reading my last book felt that I had stressed unnecessarily the sadness of our work. And now he will be feeling so again, so I must remind him of St. Paul: "As the sufferings of Christ abound in us, also by Christ doth our comfort abound."

Much of the time we are so lighthearted about our work that we are accused of "undue levity," as a melancholy Jewish friend termed it. We are called to this work because it is our vocation. We are happy in slums and we would be unhappy in a palace. We belong where we are because God put us here. The places are like refugee camps in their hardships, but when so many in the world are living under such circumstances we would not be happy unless we so lived.

"And who can separate us from the love of Christ? Shall tribulation, or distress, or famine, or nakedness, or danger, or persecution, or the sword? . . . I am sure that neither death, nor life, nor angels,

nor principalities, nor powers, nor things present, nor things to come,
nor height, nor depth, nor any other creature, shall be able to sepa-
rate us from the love of God, which is in Christ Jesus, our Lord."

And in poverty we are rich, because "all things are ours, whether
it be . . . of this world, or life, or death, or things present, or things
to come. For all our hours, and we are Christ's and Christ is God's."

I talked to Peter about the Baltimore House of Hospitality and
asked him what he thought of the disparity between idea and practice. "What chance is there to have an orderly house for Catholic
Action under such circumstance?"

"Not enough charity has been practiced," said Peter, "to make
the poor curious of the things of the spirit. . . . We have just begun
to reintroduce the idea of the House of Hospitality. Near my home in
Lozère, near the Mediterranean, in a town of eight thousand people
there is still a hospice. They have kept up the tradition even more
than a hundred years after the French Revolution. The study of history is necessary to make people know something about traditions. It
is hard to reach the industrial minded.

"But it is good to bring to the surface the bitterness of the unemployed. It disturbs the silence. When such things come to the surface
things come to a climax. It makes for Catholic public opinion. And
Catholic public opinion is not articulate yet.

"There is a priest at Catholic University who has written books
on sociology, who used to be interested in our work, but he is not any
more. He sees the necessity of working with the state and with labor
unions. It has been a long time since these things have been done
except by the government. He thinks of organization, of pressure
groups, of rights, of justice. The greatest of these is charity, but people don't want charity. The Baltimore house was only an hour from
Washington, but there were few who came to see or hear the griev-
ance of the destitute."

Maurin was referring to Paul Hanley Furfey, a sociologist at
Catholic University, who proposed the development of a person-
alist-oriented sociology. In the introduction to his book *Fire on*

Earth, Fr. Furfey stated that the best example of practical personalism was the Catholic Worker movement.

Before our house was closed by the courts in Baltimore as a public nuisance, there was hearing before two judges, and two comments of theirs will long cling to my memory.

The first judge who was conducting the hearing of the complaints of neighbors against the house leaned forward confidentially and said, "Tell me frankly, how can you stand their smell?" Meaning, in this case, the smell of colored people. Father Roy, present at the hearing, sat reading his breviary in the court. He looked up over it wryly and murmured that the stable in Bethlehem doubtless smelled.

On another occasion the judge who had charge of the welfare department asked our views on state control of such relief for transients and destitute. He admitted that the state did nothing and that there was a problem, but, "If the state did take over this work, then you would not feel bound to go on with it?" he asked us.

We assured him that we believed it to be the duty of Christians to take care of their brothers, and that only when all other means had failed was it necessary for the state to step in.

"You have a wrong concept of the state," he assured us. "To me the state is the soul and conscience of the people."

Whether in the future there will be any Houses of Hospitality or farming communes, or whether the state will take over this work and not permit the exercise of personal charity, is hard to say.

Already our houses and even some of our farms are like refugee centers. They are like camps set up in the midst of class or race war. We live hand to mouth, as best as we can, and there is never quite enough to go around, never enough warmth, never enough help, never enough energy to keep clean.

But probably from the refugee camps of the future we will look back on our freedom and opportunity for personal initiative and even to the means we have had as real luxury. Already we are so much better off than the majority of the sufferers in the world today that it seems folly to talk of sacrifice.

8

The Green Revolution

⤸

Professors of an agronomic university
do not enable their students to master subjects;
they enable them to master situations. . . .
[They] do not teach their students
how to make profitable deals;
they teach them how to realize worthy ideals.
                                    —Peter Maurin

Day began the previous chapter questioning if the Houses of Hospitality were really what Maurin had in mind. Her doubts were well founded. She probably realized that with Peter's encouragement she had followed her own vision of Catholic social reform and not his. And in this biography, which is just as much about her as it is about him, she does not discuss Maurin's "Green Revolution," which lay at the core of his thought.

A biography of Maurin that did not include this vision would not be fair to Maurin or the reader. Maurin's philosophic scope went well beyond shelters, soup kitchens, and a newspaper. Those were Dorothy's strengths and aspirations, not Peter's. Maurin was a peasant with roots in the Languedoc region of Southern France. He envisioned an economic system that would include the land as integral to his vision of economy and community. Dorothy and her Catholic Worker followers paid lip service to Maurin's concept of farming communes—they even celebrated the idea in the paper—but if actions and reality remain the true judge, they never took this idea seriously. Dorothy was from the city, and American Catholicism was for the most part an urban phenomenon. Maurin came from a far different place, and from his perspective, Catholic tradition addressed a person's relation to the earth and to the life it bears. There existed in the land a call to the spiritual dimension of humanity that the bricks and mortar of the city alone could not evoke.

Dorothy Day's intellectual universe had been strongly influenced by the argument about socialism and capitalism, and she negotiated these influences within the new world of Catholic social thought that Maurin had presented to her. But Maurin, the peasant, rejected the urban-rooted gospels of both Marxism and capitalism. He believed that each of these relatively new ideas, disconnected as they were from the land, had reduced history to a brutal individualized struggle over finite things. Confined to this vision, human progress had faltered, despite the dominant myth of progress.

Those who dismissed Maurin and his ideas accused him of wanting to transport the world back to the Middle Ages, but that was not true. Maurin embraced the present. What troubled him was the philosophic vacuum that left the contemporary world fragmented and spiritless. The Middle Ages did not provide a panacea for Maurin but rather an example of greater harmony between the spiritual and material, between finite realities and infinite values. For Maurin, the Middle Ages represented not simply a historic period but rather the expression of a moral vision that could be applied to all time.

In Maurin's view, the medieval economic system was not based on profit but rather on the enhancement of the human community. This system, he wrote, was rooted in the Catholic synthesis of "Cult, Culture, and Cultivation." By "cult" he meant the fundamental beliefs that bind a society together. By

Marquette University Archives

Peter Maurin, with Fr. Pacifique Roy, Dorothy Day, and other
Catholic Workers at a retreat at Easton, 1945.

"culture" he meant the manifestation of these fundamental
beliefs through ritual. By "cultivation" he meant the development of local economic activity supported by a sound cultivation
of the land, not for profit but for subsistence.

Some scholars have criticized Maurin for his lack of origi-
nality. This may be true, but Maurin was a great synthesizer of
ideas. Those whom he cited represented a body of thought that
has yet to be fully absorbed by contemporary scholarship. Where
the majority of opinion celebrated the unprecedented material
growth of the modern age, Maurin saw unprecedented waste—
not just material, but also human. "There is no unemployment
on the land," he used to proclaim. Where most saw technology
moving the world toward greater harmony, he saw an increasing
imbalance between rich and poor, and between resources and
consumption. And where others credited the rise of good will
through the spread of liberal idealism, he saw a disintegration of
order due to the impossibility of creating a workable ethical system within an economic system based on greed.

As previously mentioned, the thinkers who most profoundly influenced Maurin were a group referred to as the "personalists." In fact, it was Maurin who introduced the work of France's leading personalist, Emmanuel Mounier, to the United States. Mounier's view of human responsibility for the environment, as with every other issue, was rooted in scripture and tradition. According to Mounier, the earth fell with Adam because it was left by God in the care of humans and shared therefore in the human destiny. Because of this responsibility, humans had an obligation to redeem the earth along with themselves. This meant using the resources of the earth only in a way that elevated these resources and, in turn, further elevated the person. One must refrain from tyrannizing the earth, Mounier maintained, for tyranny of the earth leads to tyranny over humanity.[1]

When Maurin, along with Dorothy Day, established the Catholic Worker, the capitalist world was mired in the worst economic depression ever recorded. This financial catastrophe had come as a shock to those who put their faith in material progress through liberal economic policy. But to Maurin, the Depression was a logical culmination of a valueless system motivated by nothing more than acquisitiveness. He traced the roots of this system back to the early days of mercantile capitalism, when farmers no longer produced for the local community's needs but rather for "the middleman who was only interested in buying cheap and selling dear." It was at this point, Maurin wrote, that "the functional society ceased to exist and the acquisitive society came into existence."[2] Maurin believed that through the introduction of the marketplace more emphasis was placed on production for wealth than for need, and this distorted the delicate balance between resources and their consumption.

Maurin saw the need for humanity to live in harmony with the natural environment and outlined a plan to do so, decades before intellectuals and social activists took up this concern. His observations anticipated a growing number of historians and economists who are just beginning to study not only the impact of changing forms of technology on the organization of human labor (the Marxist model) but also the impact on the land and the possibility of a sustainable economy.[3]

While many accuse contemporary environmentalists of being futurists, the most fascinating aspect of Peter Maurin's philosophy was its immediacy. He had a plan for a network of farming communes, so he urged the Catholic Worker houses across the country to begin them. In 1935, two years after the founding of the Catholic Worker office and soup kitchen in New York City, Dorothy Day, at Maurin's urging, finally began publishing his thoughts on farming communes in the *Catholic Worker*. There were two dominant themes repeated in these articles. Taken together, they outlined the economic agrarian policy of the Catholic Worker.

The first appeared in the November 1935 issue. In Peter Maurin's "Easy Essay" style it read as follows:

> It is in fact impossible
> for any culture
> to be sound and healthy without a proper regard
> for the soil,
> no matter
> how many urban dwellers
> think that their food
> comes from groceries
> and delicatessens
> or their milk from tin cans.

There had been a time, he believed, when Americans had such a healthy respect for the soil. "At the base of the American spirit," he wrote, "is the functionalism of frontier life, not the acquisitivism [*sic*] of the Chamber of Commerce." But just as life on the medieval farm had changed from functionalism to "acquisitivism," life on the American frontier had done likewise.

Just as medieval life had been disrupted by this transformation, so too had American society.

Maurin questioned many aspects of American economic life that no one dared to criticize. For example, few questioned the efficacy of the commercialization of farming after the Civil War. Farmers who balked at the process were backward rustics who would eventually learn to step to the tune of progress. The collective memory of the period records that farmers reacted to the commercialization of farming by forming the populist movement, which brought about laws that harnessed forces they couldn't control. The farmers who survived became successful businessmen. As for those who did not survive, historians gave a Darwinian shrug and collectively declared, "It's for the best." As H. Wayne Morgan concluded, "The [populist] movement was firmly in the mainstream of American reform. . . . Its great achievement was . . . to signal the passing of agriculture as the dominant element in American life."[4]

More recently, environmental historians have begun to question this judgment. Donald Worster has noted that the commercialization of farming in this country caused a radical transformation by pressing the land not merely to produce but to do so at a profit.[5] Worster concludes, "Commercial farming had the capability of creating more wealth and more nutrition than any other agro-system could produce." But the other side of that impressive success, he notes, was a "tendency to bet high against nature [and] to raise the stakes constantly in a feverish attempt to keep from folding."[6]

Maurin believed, as do current ecologists, that in the modern era the quest for productivity and profit replaced healthy concern for the soil. To counteract this, he proposed an agricultural system that began with a respect for creation, which in this case meant the soil. He believed that Catholicism, representing a philosophy rooted in the land, provided the best preparation for such a system. Maurin may have had his own French peasant tradition in mind more than the urban American Catholic of the 1930s. But on the other hand, both the French peasant and the urban American Catholics shared a religious philosophy that respected the community and the land as a basis for that community. They each offered God a sacrifice that came "from the earth and work of human hands. . . ."

The second theme that frequently appeared in Catholic Worker articles on farming communes was, "There is no unemployment on the land." Of course the converse of this statement is a truism—the fact that there will always be unemployment in an industrial capitalist society. Some who read this part of Maurin's plan called it visionary, but Fr. John Hugo, a theologian from Pittsburgh, who made his own significant intellectual contributions to the Catholic Worker synthesis, disputed this. Hugo questioned how anyone could consider a system visionary that existed as a hard reality up to modern times in most nations and that still existed among many of the more "advanced" peoples. Hugo also pointed out that the greatest achievements of culture have come from agrarian nations, and that decay of civilization accompanied the development of industrialism. The fact that many could call such a system visionary made it clear to Hugo that "a moral revolution must precede agrarianism," and that would also include a "dismantling of the capitalist system."

"A complete change, economic and moral," Hugo concluded, "is an indispensable condition for genuine reform. Agrarians were not impractical," he argued. "The impractical ones are those who think that without such [reforms] they can better the [economic] situation by some magical or legislative device." Hugo attacked the capitalist system that laid waste to both human and natural resources in its quest for profit. "If one wishes to get rid of flies it is not enough to kill them," he concluded. "One ought to also get rid of the garbage that breeds them."[7]

A few contemporary environmentalists have only begun to see the capitalist system itself as a central cause of our environmental crisis; in fact many still hope that capitalism will produce us out of the crisis. It was Peter Maurin, and other writers attracted to his philosophy, who over sixty years ago began to argue for greater harmony between our economic and our ecological systems.

Maurin would have agreed with European historian Karl Polanyi, who wrote that capitalism "was distinctive in that it was unabashedly based on a motive only rarely acknowledged as valid in the history of human societies and certainly never before raised to the level of a justification of action and behavior in everyday life, namely gain."[8]

The capitalist system degraded the earth in its quest for wealth, and in its final stages, the late nineteenth and twentieth centuries, it began to destroy what personalists would describe as the earth's most precious resource, its people. Unemployment (a relatively new word in our vocabulary) is merely another form of industrial waste of natural resources. Because of the wastefulness of its essential character, Maurin believed that modern industrial society had become a death cult, ushering in a new dark age. Maurin paraphrased in Easy Essay form another personalist philosopher, Nicholas Berdyaev, who clearly described the death wish of modern society:

> History has failed.
> There is no such thing as historical progress.
> The present is in no wise
> an improvement on the past.
> The will to power, to well being, to wealth
> triumphs over the will
> to holiness, to genius.
> The highest spiritual achievements
> belong to the poor.
> Spirituality is on the wane
> and a time of spiritual decline
> is a time of bourgeois ascendancy.

The economics of gigantism proved itself to be a failure. It promised to reduce scarcity through mass production, but mass production was in fact creating more scarcity. Although Maurin did not witness firsthand the ecological disasters rendered by industrial capitalism in recent years, his view of history enabled him to anticipate them. For this reason, he felt it essential to restructure the economic principles on which modern society had survived. He wanted to shift from a mass economy to what British economist E. F. Schumacher described as an "economy for the masses," a decentralized, regionally based economic system.[9]

Dorothy Day knew that the House of Hospitality that housed and fed the poor and served as a center for round-table discussions was only meeting part of Peter's plan. Finally in January 1936, with a large front-page headline that announced "Back to Christ Back to the Land," Dorothy Day announced the first serious attempt the Worker movement would be making to find a farm. The page began a series of articles by Dorothy, Peter, and others, which discussed the nature of the farm experience to their more than fifty thousand, mostly urban, readers. During this period of preparation, Peter Maurin wrote the following Easy Essay:

> The central conviction
> which has dominated my mind
> ever since I began to write
> and which has increased in intensity
> during the last twenty years
> is the conviction
> that the society which has lost its spiritual roots
> is a dying culture
> however prosperous
> it may appear externally.
> Consequently, the problem of social survival
> is not only
> a political or economic one.

It is above all things religious
since it is in religion
that the ultimate spiritual roots
both of society and the individual
are to be found.

Maurin believed that the farm commune would deal directly with these fundamental problems. He preferred to call the farm an "agronomic university." Borrowing a phrase from the anarchist Peter Kropotkin, he hoped that his university would be a place where workers and scholars would come together to work out in a practical way an ethical economic system based on a respect for the land. "Scholars would become Workers," he wrote, "so that Workers can become Scholars and together they would build a new economic vision." He called his idea the "Green Revolution."

Above all, he explained, the farm would be Catholic. For at the core, the commune must have a spiritually binding, life-affirming force. Members of the commune would recognize also their partnership with God and the land. As Peter Maurin wrote:

To work on a farming commune
is to cooperate with God
in the production of food.

Subsistence would also be the model. He did not intend to create a commercial farm; to do so would be to contribute to the destruction of the land. "Diversified Farming will be practiced on the commune," the *Catholic Worker* announced. "As many different kinds of crops as the climate and soil allow will be raised." There would also be a conservation of the energy of the land by rotation of crops and the use of organic compost. Later they also determined to eat only what they raised.

Subsistence farming was not an outlandish proposition, even for the twentieth century. To prove his point Maurin, in Easy Essay form, reported on the activities of a number of successful commune experiments going on across the country. Most intriguing to him was an experiment in Vermont, where a number of people had gathered to form a village commune where traditional crafts were practiced and sold and where the surrounding land provided the food. The village comprised a diverse group of businessmen, teachers, doctors, lawyers, and carpenters, and their motto was "Not a single thing will be made that is not useful."[10]

In May 1936 the *Catholic Worker* announced that they had finally found a farm. Located about two and a half miles from Easton, Pennsylvania, it lay atop a mountain where fields stretched out for twenty-eight acres overlooking a beautiful valley. The land contained orchards of peach, apple, and cherry trees. About eight acres of the land was woodland, and there were a number of buildings, all in various stages of disrepair. The farm had cost $1,000, which was paid by contributions from readers and others interested in this farm commune experiment.

The farm got off to a hopeful beginning in June, and although he only lived there sporadically, Peter Maurin's spirit and intellect permeated the project. From 1936, when the farm began, up to World War II, when the issue of pacifism began to dominate all others at the Catholic Worker, the farmers reported monthly in the *Catholic Worker* their success in trying to work out Peter Maurin's synthesis of "Cult, Culture, and Cultivation."

Taking Peter's words to heart, they delighted to report that they had resurrected the medieval custom of gleaning the fields. "In the potato field," a member wrote, "little Dan has been busy lately gleaning the potatoes not gathered when the plough turned over the field, and he has salvaged eight more bushels to add to the forty bushels already obtained in this quarter patch." In the same article it was also announced that, "We have made a pledge this fall not to cut down a single tree but to use only the dead wood which we can clear out."

Dorothy Day visited the farm frequently and often wrote the "Farm Commune" column in the paper. When she wrote, the column breathed the spirit of agrarian idealism. Peter was the philosopher, but it was Dorothy Day whose style of life and writing has remained the Catholic Worker's richest heritage.

In one article Dorothy commented on the commune's practice of naming animals and referring to them in articles as "members of the community." Dorothy explained that because they were engrossed in trying to work out their ideas about the land as a solution to the problem of unemployment, they could not help but have a personal interest in every aspect of the farm. This included describing Bessie's calf as a new member of the family or commenting on Rosie the cow's inability to accept the presence of a new cow. Comments on events apparently so trivial showed Dorothy Day at her best. She took relatively minor events and gave them a measure of profundity. And she subtly reminded readers that as Catholics trying to work out a new economy based on a sensitivity to all living things, they stood in the line of St. Francis, who allotted to animals the same Christian love he shared with all his brothers and sisters.

Dorothy also, in her distinctive manner, brought readers' attention to the damage that industrialism was doing to the land. Writing one winter from the farm, she explained, "The Farm is beautiful all the year round and exceedingly so when there are several inches of snow on the ground. The most wonderful view can be seen by looking southward over the Delaware River and the level stretch of farms of New Jersey." She then commented that the view towards Easton "is nice also but much of its beauty has been destroyed by industrialism."[11]

The farm remained a part of the Catholic Worker movement and continued to serve as a reminder of the possibility of a more efficient, gentle economic system. But the farm never replaced the city-based House of Hospitality as the center of Catholic Worker activity, and to some the farm always remained a manifestation of Peter's eccentricities rather than his genius. Nothing could be further from the truth. Maurin's clearest explanation for the farm is revealed in a long Easy Essay he wrote entitled "Irish Culture." In it he explained that after the fall of the Roman Empire, during an era often referred to as the Dark Age,

"Irish scholars formed an intellectual synthesis and a technique of action" that created the foundations of medieval Europe. In Maurin's mind, this medieval system worked. It provided a sustainable economy that was held together by a common system of belief. "And," he concluded, "the Dark Ages were not so dark because the Irish had the light." Now, due to the destructive nature of industrial capitalism, Maurin wrote

> We are now living
> in a real Dark Age,
> and one of the reasons why
> the modern age
> is so dark
> is because
> too few Irish
> have the light.

The Catholic Worker commune, by many standards a failure, continued to have significance. It demonstrated Peter's challenge to Catholic scholars on the verge of a new dark age to reinvestigate their own traditions in order to provide meaningful dialogue with others outside of the Catholic tradition who were sincerely trying to alter the destructive nature of the economy. Peter never wanted to call the farm a commune; his word was "agronomic university," a place where new ideas could be worked out on tried principles. In Maurin's mind, the Catholic medieval system worked, and he believed it might have been the only truly functional economic system that Europe ever produced.

Agronomic universities never became the integral part of the Catholic Worker movement that Maurin had hoped. Those who joined the Catholic Worker (for the most part urban Catholics with urban concerns) saw the farm as a diversion, a retreat, a place to escape the monotony of the soup kitchen, and for all the romanticizing of life on the land, few adapted to this life and fewer still really understood this aspect of Maurin's thought.

9

Peter's Digests

College professors
are specialists
who know more and more
about less and less
and if they keep on specializing
they will end
by knowing everything
about nothing.
                    —Peter Maurin

Peter read and studied constantly, and he took the meat out of the hard shells and nourished us, constantly teaching, constantly giving us the fruit of his research. Always he was bringing us sheaves of paper, on them neat digests of what he had been reading and studying. The first of these digests I can remember was Kropotkin's Fields Factories and Workshops. I still have that little sheaf of quotations now arranged with headings and subheadings, neatly written in slanting, printed script in what is called "phrased writing."[1]

And, because the book has gone out of print, I shall reproduce some of the little sheaf of ideas here:

The Case of Mr. Ponce

In two and seven-tenths acres
Mr. Ponce cultivated every year

20,000 lbs of carrots
more than 20,000 lbs of onions, radishes
and other vegetables sold by weight
6,000 heads of cabbage
3,000 of cauliflower
5,000 baskets of tomatoes
5,000 dozen of choice fruit,
154,000 heads of salad,
in short a total of 250,000 lbs of vegetables.

1000 Acres for 1000 People

It is utterly impossible
to foresee at the present moment
what are the limits
as to the maximum number of human beings
who could draw their means of subsistence
from a given acre of land
or as to what a variety of produce
they could advantageously grow
in any latitude.

Each day widens former limits
and opens new and wide horizons.

All we can say now is
that even now
600 persons could easily live
on a square mile.
And that with cultural methods
already used in a large scale
1,000 human beings
—not idlers—
living on 1,000 acres
could easily

without any kind of over work
obtain from that acre
a luxurious vegetable and animal food,
as well as the flax, wool, silk and hides
necessary for their clothing.

The Jersey Peasants

The small island of Jersey,
eight miles long
and less than six miles wide,
still remains a land of open field culture.

Although it comprises only 28,707 acres,
rocks included,
it nourishes a population
of about two inhabitants to each acre
or 1,300 inhabitants to the square mile.

There is not one writer on agriculture
who, after having paid a visit to this island,
did not praise the well-being
of the Jersey peasants
and the admirable results
which they obtain
in their small farms
of from five to twenty acres
—very often less than five acres—
by means of a rational
and intensive agriculture.

Jersey's Economy

The successes accomplished in Jersey
are not entirely due

> to the amount of labor
> which a dense population
> is putting in the land.
>
> It is due to a system of land tenure,
> land transference, and inheritance,
> very different from those
> which prevail everywhere.
>
> It is due to freedom from State taxation.
>
> It is due to the fact
> that communal institutions
> have been maintained
> down to quite a recent period
> while a number of communal habits
> and customs of mutual support
> are alive at the present time.

One can imagine with what delight this Frenchman, this theorist, who was also a peasant, read aloud to us such excerpts as these. None of us could help but fall under the spell of such statistics. Here we were living in a crowded tenement house apartment, which looked out, it is true, on a garden and a tree, but with the hunger all of us had for something of our own. "Property is proper to man," Peter used to say. "A certain amount of property is necessary for a man to lead a good life." This was from St. Thomas.

I had lived on the seashore and had boasted of my twenty-five foot frontage, enough soil for a garden of vegetables and flowers. That soil to me was holy. I owned it. Manny Granich, who worked in the Communist Party and spent part of his time in China, came down and bought another beach bungalow, he and his wife, and they too loved the soil. I knew of other Communists who tried to get a toehold on the land for themselves and their families. How much longing there is in every human heart for a nest of their own, soil of their own. It is part of the instinct for self-preservation, I suppose.

The following are other "phrased writings" or Easy Essays written by Maurin that did not appear in Day's biography. They are included here to give further insight into Maurin's philosophic synthesis. Interspersed within these essays Maurin drops names such as Kropotkin, Harmel, Tawney, and Sorel, among others. He did this to provide a bibliography for those who would like to better understand the source of his ideas.

Materialists All

1. The Fascists
   do not believe in Marxism.

2. The Marxists
   do not believe in Capitalism.

3. The Capitalists
   do not believe in a
   Land and Crafts society.

4. But if we had
   a Land and Crafts society
   we would not have
   Capitalism.

5. And if we did not have
   Capitalism
   we would not have
   Marxism.

6. And if we did not have
   Marxism
   we would not have Fascism.

7. So to foster
    a Land and Crafts society
    is to fight
    Capitalism, Marxism, Fascism.

Blowing the Dynamite

Writing about the Catholic Church
a radical writer says:
"Rome will have to do more
than to play a waiting game;
she will have to use
some of the dynamite
inherent in her message."
To blow the dynamite
of a message
is the only way
to make the message dynamic.

If the Catholic Church
is not today
the dominant social dynamic force,
it is because Catholic scholars
have failed to blow the dynamite
of the Church.

Catholic scholars
have taken the dynamite
of the Church,
have wrapped it up
in nice phraseology,
placed it in an hermetic container
and sat on the lid.

It is about time
to blow the lid off
so the Catholic Church
may again become
the dominant social dynamic force.

Out of the Temple

Christ drove the money changers
out of the Temple.
But today nobody dares
to drive the money lenders
out of the Temple.
And nobody dares
to drive the money lenders
out of the Temple
because the money lenders
have taken a mortgage
on the Temple.

When the church builders build churches
with money borrowed from money lenders
they increase the prestige
of the money lenders.

But increasing the prestige
of the money lenders
does not increase the prestige
of the Church.
Which makes Archbishop McNichols say:
"We have been guilty
of encouraging tyranny
in the financial world
until it has become

a veritable octopus
strangling the life
of our people."

Ethics and Economics

Lincoln Steffens says:
"The social problem
is not a political problem
it is an economic problem."

Kropotkin says:
"The economic problem
is not an economic problem
it is an ethical problem."

Thorstein Veblen says:
"There are no ethics
in modern society."

R. H. Tawney says:
"There were high ethics
in society
when the Canon Law
was the law of the land."
The high ethics
of the Canon Law
are embodied in the encyclicals
of Pius XI and Leo XIII
on the social problem.
To apply the ethics
of the encyclicals
to the problems of today,
such is the purpose
of Catholic Action.

When Civilizations Decay

When the bank account
is the standard of values
the class on the top
sets the standard.
When the class on the top
cares only for money
it does not care for culture,
nobody cares for culture.
And when nobody cares
for culture
civilization decays.

Church and State

Modern society believes
in separation
of Church and State.
But the Jews
did not believe in it,
the Greeks
did not believe in it,
the Medievalists
did not believe in it,
the Puritans
did not believe in it.
Modern Society
has separated
the Church from the State,
but it has not separated
the State from business.
Modern Society

does not believe
in a Church's State;
it believes
in a business men's State.
"And it is the first time
in the history of the world
that the State is controlled
by businessmen,"
says James Truslow Adams.

To the Bishops of the U.S.A.

People who are in need
and are not afraid to beg
give to people not in need
the occasion to do good
for goodness' sake.
Modern society calls the beggar
bum and panhandler
and gives him the bum's rush.
But the Greeks used to say
that people in need
are the ambassadors of the gods.
Although you may be called
bums and panhandlers
you are in fact the Ambassadors of God.
As God's Ambassadors
you should be given food,
clothing and shelter
by those who are able to give it.
Mohametan teachers tell us
that God commands hospitality,
and hospitality is still practiced
in Mohametan countries.

But the duty of hospitality
is neither taught nor practiced
in Christian countries.

Houses of Hospitality

We need Houses of Hospitality
to give the rich
the opportunity to serve the poor.
We need Houses of Hospitality
to bring the Bishops to the people
and the people to the Bishops.
We need Houses of Hospitality
to bring back to institutions
the technique of institutions.
We need Houses of Hospitality
to show what idealism looks like
when it is practiced.
We need Houses of Hospitality
to bring social justice
through Catholic Action
exercised in Catholic Institutions.

Hospices

We read in the *Catholic Encyclopedia*
that during the early ages of Christianity
the hospice (or House of Hospitality)
was a shelter for the sick, the poor,
the orphans, the old, the traveler,
and the needy of every kind.
Originally the hospices (or
Houses of Hospitality)
were under the supervision of the Bishops,

who designated priests
to administer the spiritual
and temporal affairs
of these charitable institutions.
The fourteenth statute
of the so-called Council of Carthage,
held about 436,
enjoins upon the Bishops
to have hospices (or Houses of Hospitality)
in connection with their churches.

Parish Houses of Hospitality

Today we need Houses of Hospitality
as much as we needed them then,
if not more so.
We have Parish Houses for priests,
Parish Houses for education purposes,
Parish Houses for recreational purposes,
But no Parish Houses of Hospitality.
Bossuet says that the poor
are the first children of the Church
so the poor should come first.
We need parish Homes
as well as Parish Domes.

Houses of Catholic Action

Catholic Houses of Hospitality
should be more than free guest houses
for the Catholic unemployed.
They could be vocational training schools,
including the training for the priesthood,
as Father Corbett proposes.

They could be Catholic reading rooms,
as Father McSorley proposes . . .
They could be Roundtable Discussion Groups,
as Peter Maurin proposes.
In a word they could be
Catholic Action Houses,
where Catholic Thought
is combined with Catholic Action.

Reconstructing the Social Order

The Holy Father and the Bishops ask us
to reconstruct the social order.
The social order was once constructed
through dynamic Catholic Action.
When the barbarians invaded
the decaying Roman Empire
Irish Missionaries went all over Europe
and laid the foundations of Medieval Europe
through the establishment of
cultural centers,
that is to say Round Table Discussions.
They brought thought to the people.
through free guest houses,
that is to say, Houses of Hospitality.
They popularized the divine
virtue of charity
through farming colonies,
that is to say, Agronomic Universities.
They emphasized voluntary poverty.
It was on the basis of personal charity
and voluntary poverty
that Irish Missionaries
laid the foundations
of the social order.

Wealth Producing Maniacs

When John Calvin
legalized moneylending
at interest
he made the bank account
the standard of values.
When the bank account
became the standard of values
people ceased
to produce for use
and began
to produce for profits.
When people began
to produce for profits
they became
wealth-producing maniacs.
When people became
wealth-producing maniacs
they produced
too much wealth.
When people found out
that they had produced
too much wealth
they went on an orgy
of wealth destruction
and destroyed
ten million lives besides.
And fifteen years after
a world-wide orgy
of wealth and life
destruction
millions of people
find themselves victims

of a world-wide depression
brought about
by a world gone mad
on mass-production
and mass-distribution.

A Second Letter to Father Lord S.J.

There is a lot of talk today
about the social value of Fascism.
But Fascism is only a stopgap
between capitalism and Bolshevism.
Fascist dictatorship is a half-way house
between the rugged individualism of capitalism
and the rugged collectivism of Bolshevism.
There is no essential difference
between Fascist dictatorship
and Bolshevik dictatorship.
The trouble with the world today is
too much dictatorship
and too little leadership.

Catholic laymen and women
commit the great modern error
of separating the spiritual
from the material.
This great modern error,
known under the name secularism,
is called a modern plague
by Pope Pius XI. . . .

We are threatened with
dynamic Bolshevik action
because we are sorely lacking
in dynamic Catholic Action.

The Age of Chaos

And we are now
in the age of chaos.
In an age of chaos
people look
for a new order.
Because people are becoming aware
of this lack of order
they would like to be able
to create order
out of chaos.
The time
to create order
out of chaos
is now.
The germ of the present
was in the past
and the germ of the future
is in the present.
The thing to do
is to give up old tricks
and start to play new tricks.

The Age of Order

If we make
the right decisions
in the age of chaos
the effect of those decisions
will be a better order.
The new order
brought about

by right decisions
will be functional,
not acquisitive;
personalist,
not socialist;
communitarian,
not collectivist;
organismic,
not mechanistic.
The thing to do right now
is to create a new society
within the shell of the old
with the philosophy of the new
which is not a new philosophy
but a very old philosophy,
a philosophy so old
that it looks like new.

Pie in the Sky

Bourgeois capitalists
don't want their pie
in the sky
when they die.
They want their pie
here and now.
To get their pie
here and now
bourgeois capitalists
give us
better and bigger
commercial wars
for the sake of markets
and raw materials.

But as Sherman says,
"War is hell."
So we get hell
here and now
because bourgeois capitalists
don't want their pie
in the sky
when they die,
but want their pie
here and now.

Bolshevik Socialists,
like bourgeois capitalists
don't want their pie
in the sky
when they die.
They want their pie
here and now.
To get their pie
here and now,
Bolshevik Socialists
give us
better and bigger
class wars
for the sake
of capturing the control
of the means of production
and distribution.

But war is hell,
whether it is
a commercial war
or a class war.
So we get hell
here and now

because Bolshevik Socialists
don't want their pie
in the sky
when they die,
but want their pie
here and now.

Bolshevik Socialists
as well as
bourgeois capitalists
give us hell
here and now
without
leaving us the hope
of getting our pie
in the sky
when we die.
We just
get hell.

Catholic Communionism
leaves us the hope
of getting our pie
in the sky
when we die
without
giving us hell
here and now.

Class-Consciousness

Georges Sorel thought
that violence
is the midwife

of existing societies.
When the employers
believe in violence
the workers also
believe in it.
Class consciousness
among employers
brings class-consciousness
among the workers.
To do away
with class struggle
we must first of all
do away
with class-consciousness
among employers.

The workers are what
the employers make them.
When employers
are moved by greed
the workers are inclined
to carry a grudge.

Harmel on Proper Use of Property

Leon Harmel,
who was an employer,
not a labor leader
says: "We have lost
the right concept of authority
since the Renaissance."
We have not only lost
the right concept of authority,
we have also lost

the right concept of property.
The use of property
to acquire more property
is not the proper use
of property.
The right use of property
is to enable the worker
to do his work
more effectively.
The right use of property
is not to compel the worker
under the threat of unemployment
to be a cog in the wheel
of mass production.

Catholics Need to Return to the Land

Ralph Adams Cram says:
"What I propose
is that Catholics
should take up
this back-to-the-land problem
and put it into operation.
Why Catholics?
Because they realize
more clearly than any others
the shortcomings
of the old capitalist
industrial system.
They, better than others,
see the threat
that impends.
They alone understand
that while the family

is the primary social unit,
the community comes next.
And there is
no sound
and righteous
and enduring community
where all its members
are not substantially
of one mind
in matters of the spirit—
that is to say,
of religion."

10

A Good Man

◈

To give and not to take,
  that is what makes man human.
To serve and not to rule,
  that is what makes man human.
To help and not to crush,
  that is what makes man human.
To nourish and not to devour,
  that is what makes man human.
And if need be, to die and not to live,
  that is what makes man human.
  —Peter Maurin

Peter Maurin often said that the purpose of the Catholic Worker was "to work for the kind of society where it would be easier for people to be good." In this final chapter, Dorothy Day reflects on the meaning of Peter Maurin's life, or rather the meaning his life had for her, and struggles with the challenge of describing a man who was "truly good." It is an important reflection, because as it turned out, his words and actions put Day's life onto a path that would take her from a pious Christian convert, quietly living out her commitment, to becoming the most dynamic and influential American Catholic in the twentieth century. Day's reputation is measured in terms of influence and respect. But as Day reflects on the life of Maurin, she reveals that it was his meekness that attracted her—a virtue not normally celebrated by those who, in history's judgment, have significance or importance. However, Maurin's "meekness" was for neither the fainthearted nor the cowardly. It was the meekness of Christ, who permitted himself to be betrayed by friends, spat upon by soldiers, and yet created a revolution in the world that shaped a new moral paradigm.

Had Christ himself come to Dorothy Day, the change in her life would have been no more radical. For in Peter she saw Christ. A man of the spirit, a man who had a vision of the eternal, and a determination to bring that vision to the Lower East Side of New York, or to wherever else his travels would take him. His idea was simple, yet thoroughly baffling for most of those who heard him. The world was in a terrible mess, Maurin believed. The world could move away from that terrible crisis if people would accept the simple truth of the Incarnation. To Maurin this doctrine was not a theological abstraction. It simply meant that God had come to earth to show humans how they ought to live. Those who chose that example found peace, for they were bringing the eternal closer to harmony with the temporal. To Maurin, poverty, social conflict, war could all be traced to the fact that collective memory, which determines future direction, had edited the eternal out of the human story. Maurin, through his Easy Essays, tried to reintegrate the eternal into the human experience. He did not simply preach that life, he lived it. He literally, as Dorothy Day used to say, "put on Christ."

The problem I have to face in writing this book is to present the picture of a truly good man, a Christ-like man, and to show him as he is, human, sympathetic, and warm. One of the ways of doing this is to admit faults, to show up little imperfections, if only to point out more clearly the rare virtues of the man.

I read recently a book of commentaries on the work of Dosto-

evsky, the writer who has most influenced my life, and there is a chapter devoted to this problem of how to present a truly good man, a Christ-like man. My notebook is filled with quotations from Dostoevsky's letters and notes, and since I too am trying to portray the life, the character of a truly good man, I want to reproduce them here.

According to Ernest J. Simmons, "The moral force of meekness and passive humility was to become a major factor in much of Dostoevsky's later theorizing, and its importance in his fiction is evidenced by the series of great characters that followed. All of these characters demonstrate the powerful social message of Christ, that the meek shall inherit the earth."

Peter is not a reader of Dostoevsky, but the fact that I have always been such a student of the Russian has helped me to understand Peter, and to understand him as one of the meek, whom Dostoevsky loved to portray.

We have such wrong concepts of meekness, and I wonder if among us, English-speaking people, the word "meek" has not come to be associated with the Uriah Heeps of the world, and to be accepted as a cowardly virtue. What does the word mean? Some would say that it is recognition of our dependence on Christ; that we are but dust. On the other hand we have the dignity of being sons of God. The word "humility" comes from humus, dirt. Everything we look upon comes from dirt, from the earth. The chair we sit in, whether metal or wooden, the table we write at, the machine we use, the paper and ink, the food we eat, the clothes we wear, our body—blood, bone, and tissue—all comes from the earth. "Dust thou art and to dust thou shalt return." And yet God has made us a little less than the angels. He has made us in his image and likeness. And he has made us his sons.

So again the Christian virtue of meekness and humility is a paradoxical one. We are meek but we are the sons of God. "I can do all things in him," and on the other hand, without him nothing.

Certainly, Peter's dignity does not consist in possessions. He possesses literally nothing, and what he happens to have at this moment anyone can take. Such is his meekness. Peter quotes sadly in relation to the family and the farm:

"Cursed is the earth in thy work; with labor and toil shalt thou eat thereof all the days of thy life. Thorns and thistles shall it bring forth to thee; and thou shalt eat the herbs of the earth. In the sweat of thy face shalt thou eat bread till thou return to the earth, out of which thou wast taken. For dust thou art and unto dust shalt thou return."

All of which explains why men are loath to work, why it goes against the grain, why it is so difficult to find a philosophy of labor among them. But it does not answer the question as to what we shall do about it. How much are we responsible for the care of our brother? How much do we contribute in his delinquency by our meekness? How far should meekness go? And our Peter quotes again the question St. Peter asked of our Lord, "How many times shall I forgive my brother? Seven times?" And the Lord answered him, "Till seventy times seven."

And the answer of the apostles to this is, "Lord, increase our faith." Our faith in our brothers, our faith in God's love for our brothers, and our enemies.

But the murmurers keep saying, "How long, O Lord, how long should we let them get away with it? When does freedom and liberty degenerate into license? When are we going to have a proper concept of authority and freedom? When are we going to have a right social order?"

In the story of the prodigal son, for instance, his father welcomed him back that time. But how many times is he supposed to kill the fatted calf for him? Undoubtedly few reforms are lasting. There are not many sudden and complete conversions like that of St. Mary Magdalene and St. Augustine. The just man falls seven times daily.

What a world problem, this authority and freedom, and the tension between the two! And how we Americans have held onto the Christian ideas of freedom and the dignity of human personality while forgetting that freedom is based on complete submission, complete meekness to God.

Because the farm is a permanent community many of our basic problems show up there. Peter did not most certainly intend Houses of Hospitality on the land, yet many a time in summer the farm becomes just such a House of Hospitality, a children's camp, a workers' school. People come and stay for vacations and long visits.

One summer, years ago, we were most crowded; there was scarcely food enough to go around. A few of those in charge had contracted the bad habit of charging, and the bills were piling up. There was little recognition of what voluntary poverty or Christian asceticism meant. There was no acceptance of Peter's slogan, "Raise what you eat and eat what you raise." Still people were always kicking about the food. We had a goodly number of chickens, to which we fed laying mash. Again we were going against fundamental principles. We should have raised all the chicken food ourselves or done without chickens.

But again a principle of authority came in. Having delegated the authority to another, the so-called manager of the farming commune, he was to be left at liberty to try to work things out, and learn by working, to learn by mistakes, to learn by free discussions among the group at the farm. There was no such thing as majority rule. The farm manager, like a medieval abbot, could rule, and the others had to accept his rule. There could be discussions; but there could be no vote. Perhaps the others could change his mind if he were making mistakes, by persuasion or discussion. But otherwise they had to submit and let things take their course and trust to time and to God to straighten out mistakes. Such a philosophy of administration calls for infinite patience. But it is the policy that has been in use in Benedictine communities the world over since St. Benedict's day. (But Benedictines come together for religious reasons by choice, not by compulsion or economic necessity or sickness. When they were motivated by baser ideas the community was anything but a success.)

Our point of view, though the Christian one, calls for so many explanations that it is hard to get to the point of a very small story, illustrating Peter's meekness, that I am trying to tell.

One summer day there was a fight over an egg. Usually there

were enough eggs for each member of the community to have one that could be eaten at breakfast or lunch. On one occasion one of the men, an ex-soldier, put his egg to one side to eat later. When he came in at lunch time it was gone, and he accused the cook, a French Canadian textile worker, of stealing it. This contention led to blows and Louis knocked the cook down.

Peter was a witness to this fight. He has so complete a hatred of the use of force that he paled. Perhaps it was with wrath—"the righteous wrath with no undue desire of revenge," of which St. Thomas speaks. But Peter did have his revenge. "Since there is not enough to go around," he said firmly, "I'll do without both milk and eggs for the rest of the summer."

The bickering over the food did not cease, however. This self-denial of Peter's led to another discussion that lasted all summer, a discussion as to whether justice comes before charity or after. Those who were holding the position that justice comes first were the most avid to get their share of everything and the last ones to practice self-denial. Justice comes first, they always said firmly, and they are still saying it to this day. Which leads many to say, "You see your emphasis on freedom does not work. You need rules and regulations to enforce order."

All over the world they are discussing these ideas, and at this moment chaos reigns. People say "We will give up our freedom to bring about freedom," and "We do evil that good may come of it. We must hate, we must use superior force to that of the enemy. If he uses poison gas so must we. We will show him that we are tougher, stronger, more ruthless, more relentless." In other words, the militant Christian virtues are to the fore. We will win the war first and talk about Christianity afterward. Justice comes before charity.

Peter believed the only way to lead was by example; the only way to organize others was to organize yourself. In the face of this meekness, let us see Peter's own schedule for the day. A grueling schedule, a typical peasant's schedule of hard work. I found it neatly lettered on the back of his missal.

Daily Schedule

5 to 7	Work in Field
7 to 9	Mass
9 to 10	Breakfast (some discussion and reading)
10 to 11	Lecture or Discussion
11 to 2	Rest or Study
2 to 3	Lecture or Discussion
3 to 4	Cold Lunch
4 to 5	Lesson in Handcraft
5 to 8	Work in Field
8 to 9	Dinner
9 to 5	Sleep

On the farm Peter kept pretty faithfully to the early-to-bed, early-to-rise idea, but the discussions went on at night too. In the city it is harder to sleep early in the evening. In the summer the neighborhood comes to life at night, and there is talk and radios and fighting until midnight so that it is hard to read or rest. And in the winter there are always meetings to attend so that one comes home late, and there were discussions in Peter's library which lasted until all hours, so that though his rising time was constant between ten and eleven there was no telling when he would go to bed.

Take one winter for instance. There were not only his meetings, but there was his desire "to make a point." It was almost the death of Peter this time, but he made his point all right.

Always around a newspaper office there are many visitors who are cranks, and just as we ourselves feel that we have the solution for the world's ills, so do they, and they wish to be listened to. There are the perfectly sane ones, like the single-taxers who disapprove of our charity and feel that we are wasting our time unless we get busy with the tax and ownership reforms that they advocate. There are the "arts and crafts" groups who never tire of droning into our ears, "If they don't work neither shall they eat." There are the cooperative

Marquette University Archives

groups who feel that the paper should be devoted from beginning to end to stories about cooperation and world reform. And our friends look pityingly on us and say, "Poor Dorothy, poor Peter, they are all right, of course, but they do things the hard way." Or they say, "Poor Peter, what a hash Dorothy has made of his ideas with her sentimental philanthropies."

Most of these visitors are so busy, their lives are so filled, that they do not bother to take too much of our time. Indeed it is hard to pin them down to speaking for an evening meeting or leading a discussion or teaching a class for them, because all want to be teachers or leaders, not listeners or followers.

Then there are all the freedom groups and their propagandists, followers of seemingly lost causes, patriots, nationalists, as well as believers in world brotherhood. Mexicans, Italians, Spaniards, Poles, Russians, Indians, all manner of friends of freedom gather together to tell us what this or that group is doing.

Then there are the prisoners. Throughout the country there have been men imprisoned for their work in the labor movement, accused of murder, arson, sabotage. They are of all political faiths, from IWWs, to Communists, to plain trade unionists. And for each man or group of men imprisoned, there are committees and groups pledged to get them out, and these come to tell their story and to ask for space in the paper, even though ours is only an eight-page tabloid appearing once a month. Because of our friends, because of the size of our circulation, we are respected.

Then there are the poor, who come to us hungry and homeless and ill-clad, and these can be dealt with immediately, even if it means taking off one's coat and warming them. One can always raise a plate of soup and a cup of hot coffee and some bread. That is how our bread lines started. We never planned to be running bread lines. We never planned to have so large a family staying with us. They just grew up around us. And it is not as though we could devote our whole attention to them, what with the paper, the correspondence, visitors, writings, etc. But people are the most importunate thing in our lives, and these poor ones, our brothers. So paper, writing, correspondence, visitors all are sacrificed to them.

The paper may stop publication. Half our houses are closed due to war-time decline of unemployment and lack of people to run them. But the ideas live and the houses will spring up again, we are sure, come what may, so that we will again be living in these self-same groups as long as we live. And always living with us and sharing with us will be some "friends of the family," some "ambassadors of Christ," some "honest thieves."

Hardest of all to deal with are those who have gone off the deep end and whose brains have collapsed completely. There are always a few of these in our midst.

There was Edleson, the Jew, who could recite psalms to us in Hebrew, who had so passionate a devotion to the Blessed Mother that he wore a rosary around his neck. There was C, the poet, who wrote poems like Poe, who was blond and impressive, and who stood for hours in the middle of the floor "caught in a cold air pocket," he used to say. Peter brought him to us one evening, and for several years he lived with us, deranged though he was.

There are men and women with persecution complexes who believe that people in the government are discriminating against them or who have other mild phobias in regard to their neighbors. There was a woman with whom I shared an apartment in the house who use to sit in the rocking chair with a wet towel folded and tied to her mouth and around her head. She was sure there was poison gas in the air. There was another women who wore a tall wig, whose skin was bright yellow, who sat on the stairs between meals and talked to an imaginary lover. There is right now a young woman unspeakably filthy and in rags who wanders the streets by night and sleeps in the church around the corner during the day and sings and laughs when you talk to her and seems radiantly happy always.

One time Smitty came to me and said, "She is always getting fresh clothes. She is lousy, and once a week she comes in to get another outfit. I've given her four coats already, and she takes her clothes off and drops them right there, and dresses right in front of me. It is very embarrassing."

But the hardest of all to deal with are the madmen who come with panaceas for the social order in their pockets. Perfectly serious, they will sit down beside my desk and take out of their briefcases curious scrolls with colored charts and symbols and unroll them before you and start to tell you that theirs is the mighty brain that we have been waiting for to direct the work. They have come to teach, and they complain that no one will listen.

I have talked to at least three of these men during the last three months. I have tried to get one of the men—a young fellow who used to belong to a religious order—to go to a clinic. E is young, perhaps there is a possibility of his being cured of his mental illness, but as soon as I start talking about visiting a clinic he flees. The others are men who wander the streets and talk interminably to their fellows and are never listened to.

Doubtless we have not been as patient as we should have been. It is true that after fifteen minutes or so we plead business engagements, and find some way to get rid of them.

But one winter Peter took upon himself the care of these unfortunates. Two of them became his constant visitors, and hour after hour they kept him in the library, talking, scolding, criticizing, wearing him down little by little.

We used to try to rescue him. We were quite unscrupulous, summoning him to the telephone, taking him away on imaginary appointments. But he insisted upon bearing with his unwanted guests.

For three months in the spring I was traveling on the West Coast, visiting our houses out there. When I came back this game was still going on. Peter was a shadow of his former self. His face was drawn and gray, his voice slow, and he could not remember proper names. As soon as I returned from my trip and saw his condition, I took him to a friend of mine, a German doctor. She had spent a year in Hitler's concentration camps for refusing to sterilize epileptic children. Her husband is a Jew and had reached America first and raised money here to ransom her from the camp. She has a ready sympathy for our work and understands it as few do, so it was a pleasure to go to her with our troubles.

Peter answered her questions truthfully. She took his blood pressure, listened to his heart, and questioned him. I told her about his visitors, who kept him up until two or three every night in a hot stuffy room dinning into his ears their insane ramblings.

He looked at me pleadingly, "But they are driven from pillar to post. No one will listen to them. I was trying to find out what they are trying to say."

And trying, too, I thought to myself, to impress upon our minds by his extreme remedy, the need for us to show patience, to listen, to try to understand what they are trying to say.

His only admission was that they kept him from thinking. And to Peter, the thinker, who walked the streets pondering over human problems, who sat by the hour meditating in church, who valued his long hours of quiet as he did his hours of conversation, to be kept from thinking must have been torture.

Peter never quite recovered his health after that. A few years later he awoke one morning with memory gone and bodily strength enfeebled. He has remained an invalid since.

Dostoevsky wrote, "Don Quixote and Pickwick as virtuous figures succeeded in gaining sympathy of the reader because they are laughable." But if the hero in his novel The Idiot is not laughable, "then he has another appealing feature, his innocence." Prince Myshkin is described as entirely passive. He willingly accepts suffering, is easily put upon, answers offenses by begging forgiveness, and exaggerates the good in others while constantly overlooking evil. Dostoevsky describes submissiveness as "the most fearful force that can exist in the world."

Certainly Peter, with all his sureness as to the efficacy of his program for the new social order, was the most meek and submissive of men. I have seen him again and again at meetings cut short by the chairman with no sign of resentment, even when he had been stopped in the middle of a word. He would just say, "Oh," in a little apologetic tone, and take his seat. He neither took offense nor bore resentment. He continued to bring his message to those who would listen. He was entirely unsuspicious and never thought ill of anyone. On the contrary, he saw their good points to so extravagant an extent that his friends would say indulgently, "He has no judgment in regard to people."

On the other hand, a certain Mother Foundress said to her sisters, "One sign of perfection is not to notice the imperfections of others." It is not that Peter looked upon all people equally with the same friendliness and warmth. No, he had his preferences (just as our Lord had for John), and many of us were irked by his almost fantastic expectancies in regard to this program or that. "What can he see in them?" we said to each other in wonder. Doubtless there was a bit of jealousy in our irked impatience. "They are all right, they are brilliant perhaps in their intelligence, but truly there is nothing extraordinary in either their accomplishments or in their promise for the future." But Peter loved them as sons and brothers, and told of their accomplishments and attributes with enthusiastic joy to all his other friends and listeners. (None of the three he especially loved have come near him in his illness.)

There was something quite childlike in this hopefulness, in this enthusiasm; and how beautiful an attribute always to see the good!

And as for Peter being uncomplaining!

One week in February the weather became bitterly cold. It was below zero and it got to the point in our houses, heated only by old-fashioned oil stoves or open grates, that we went partly dressed to bed. We quoted St. Vincent Ferrer to justify our sloth: he never completely disrobed, considering it a waste of time. And of course there are the Trappists who go winter and summer in the same garb and sleep in their robes. But we were rebelling against the cold, not accepting it as they did. We went to bed in woolen stockings, sweaters, and even scarves around our heads. There were not enough blankets to go around and the cold seemed to settle in one's bones.

"Are you warm enough?" I asked Peter one morning as we huddled around the oil stove in the office.

"No," he answered matter-of-factly. And when I went back to the library after he had left for church I examined his bed. He had it neatly made up with the spread pulled up, but there was nothing under the spread. Someone had taken his blankets, and he was sleeping in his clothes under his overcoat and leaving the oil burner going all night to keep warm.

Though he answered when queried, he never commented on the weather, whether it was hot or cold, whether it was wet or dry, whether he felt ill or well, hungry or thirsty. Truly his speech was "yea, yea, nay, nay." It was to the point.

While I write these pages my heart glows within me, and I feel joyfully how happy this book is going to make many of our friends.

"They will thank me, they will be grateful," I say to myself as I write, *"just as thankful as I am to Peter."*

The infant leaped with joy in the womb of Elizabeth at the salutation of Mary, bearing the Lord. So we feel when we encounter one of Christ's friends.

"Was not our heart burning within us whilst he spoke along the way?" These are the words of two of the disciples at Emmaus, who sat down to dine with their fellow traveler, and *"they knew him in the breaking of the bread."*

Peter has taught us to know each other, to see Christ in each other, in the breaking of the bread. He has taught us the joy and life-giving qualities of the works of mercy. He has brought to us Christ in the poor, as surely as the Blessed Mother brought Christ to Elizabeth. He has shown us the way, with his poverty and his works of mercy, and that way is Christ.

* * *

Peter is no longer with us. He is not dead, but his mind is tired, he says. He cannot think. He has long had a heart condition, and it has led to hardening of the arteries of the brain. He lives with us on our farm, which is run as a retreat house at Newburgh, New York, and he no longer talks, no longer teaches. He reads a little, but he finds that tiring. He listens a little to the retreats, to the visitors, but he cannot listen long. His mind is tired. He gets up in the morning with the rest, goes to prime, the morning prayer of the Church, and to mass, and Holy Communion. He eats with us, and he is always hungry. We wonder if he is remembering lean years in France, when a family of twenty-three or so never had quite enough to go around. In between meals, in the summer, he sits on the porch in the sun and reads and drowses. In the winter he sits by the fire. Sometimes he does not know what time it is, what day it is. Sometimes he comes down from compline, the evening prayer, and thinks it is time for breakfast. One time, when he was in New York, he even got lost. For three days we searched the streets, the Bowery, and the hospitals for him. For three days we listened for his slow step on the stairs, the sound of his cough or the door opening. He had wandered out for a little walk and had gotten lost. And we wondered with a dreadful constriction of the heart, whether this was the way Peter Maurin was going to end. Was he, the poor man, going to wander out on the streets and disappear, lost and forgotten, perhaps put as dead storage in the vast mental hospitals such as we have in New York State, where fifteen thousand inmates sit around in wards all day, every day of the year many of them, just because they have lost their memory? And we would never find him?

But he came back, thank God; he came in smiling his radiant happy smile, panting a little from exhaustion. "This place is very hard to find," he said of Mott Street, where he had lived for ten years. "I've been wandering around in buses, sitting in coffee shops."

So now we keep him at the farm, at the retreat house, and people come and go all the time, and there are new faces, new voices, and young people who are talking about old ideas. But they are ideas and programs that Peter has made new for us. "He made all things new." So that we began to see with the warm eyes of love, we began to see Christ in each other, and we began to see visions and dream dreams, as in earlier days when the faith was young.

I write this sad news now about Peter, so that while you read, you do not begin to glow and say, "I'll make a pilgrimage, I'll go see this man," and then be disappointed. We've seen that happen. Joe Connell came back from the wars. He had come across copies of the Catholic Worker in a hospital in France, and had read Peter's writings and made up his mind to come back to sit at his feet, to learn from him, and to try to remake his life. "It is a time for the absolute," he kept saying when he got back. And Peter was the one he wanted to give him a concept of it.

There have been many others like that. "Is he still alive?" we are asked. "Is he still writing?" No, he no longer writes, but unlike other newspapers, we find it pertinent to reprint again and again his little essays that cast such a light on problems of the day, which are a guide in their way to the making of history. Peter has made history and is making history.

One time he was talking to three journalists who were visiting in the office and they were talking of ways to present and handle the news. No editorial comments, no slants, they agreed. But Peter insisted that journalists should make history as well as write about it. We all know how William Randolph Hearst has made it.

"Have you ever worked in a newspaper office?" one of the men asked Peter, perhaps with a touch of condescension.

"Yes, once in Chicago, I worked with the Associated Press," Peter said, "wielding a mop, not a pen."

Of course there were many who did not see Peter as he was—as a maker of history, a saint of our times. Perhaps this book will do nothing but interest them as a sort of line on one aspect of social thought. They are more used to the type of saints who, aflame with the love of God, do not see the world around them but keep their eyes fixed on eternity and so lead many to follow Christ.

But in all times, God raises up men to meet the problems. We are living in a time when Communism is sweeping slowly and steadily over Europe, as it has already spread over the one-sixth of the world that was Russia. There are gigantic changes being made in the political, social, economic setup of states. Catholics are too apt to take the line that we must follow the lesser evil, as though there were no other choices.

Is there no choice but that between Communism and industrial capitalism? Is Christianity so old that it has become stale, and is Communism the brave new torch that is setting the world afire? Strange commentary that when Catholics begin to realize their brotherhood and betake themselves to the poor and to all races, then it is that they are accused of being Communists. Catholics and Communists thrown together in concentration camps in Europe came to know one another, and God only knows what conversations came about. He works in little ways, hidden ways. What chances are there for mass conversions these days when Statism has become a heresy *that is engulfing even Catholics so that they do not realize that they are as materialistic as any Marxist?*

Peter has pointed a way, a little way, for the man in the street. He has built up a new apostolate. He has reached the poorest and the most destitute by living always among them, sharing their poverty, and sharing what he has with them. And this expression of love is rarer than one thinks.

I'm not saying that Peter is the only saint of his day. There are many saints, I am convinced, here, there, and everywhere, and not only the canonized ones that Rome calls to our attention.

Peter has a message for all, though all are certainly not called to go out as he did among the poor, as a teacher and worker. The doctor, the laboratory worker, the teacher in his classroom, the worker at his machine, the farmer at his plough, the student at his books, all have their vocations, and a different amount of this world's goods is needed for all. The doctor has need of more than the laborer—an office, a reception room, and a telephone. Poverty is a thing of the spirit as well as the flesh. But we do not see enough of Peter's kind of poverty. His message of poverty is for all, and his message of personal responsibility is for all.

* * *

Peter Maurin lived for about two more years in the deteriorated state that Day described in her manuscript. He died on Sunday, May 15, 1949. Dorothy Day had concluded her manuscript on Peter Maurin before that date, but she described his death and funeral in her autobiography, *The Long Loneliness*, which she published in 1952.

Peter had been sitting up for supper that Sunday night and had been out in the sun all afternoon. There had been visitors from Friendship House, and on Saturday Ludwinne von Kersbergen from Grailville had been at the farm, and had told Peter with love and reverence all he had meant to the lay apostolate throughout the world. It was like a benediction from Europe. She might indeed have been representing Europe at that moment in saying farewell to him. His writings have been published there; he has been recognized there, as perhaps he never has in this his adopted country.

At eleven that night, Peter began coughing, and it went on for some minutes. He then tried to rise, and fell over on his pillow, breathing heavily. Hans put on the light and called Fr. Faley and Jane. Michael, Eileen, and others came too, and there were prayers for the dying about the bedside. He died immediately; there was no struggle, no pain.

He was laid out at Newburgh the first night, in the conference room where he sat so often trying to understand the discussions and the lectures. Flowers were all about him from shrubs in our garden and from our neighbors. He wore a suit that had been sent in for the poor. The next morning he was brought to Mott Street and laid out at the end of the store we used for an office.

All that day and night people came from the neighborhood, from all over the city, from different parts of the country, and filled the little store and knelt before the coffin. Whenever we were sitting in the room we saw them quietly, almost secretly, pressing their rosary beads to Peter's hands. Some bent down and kissed him.

The neighbors sent beautiful floral pieces, and all around the coffin were branches of the flowering shrubs the group had sent down from Maryfarm. The sweet smells filled the room, and it was hot and fresh outside. The funeral was at nine o'clock next morning at the Salesian Transfiguration Church on Mott Street. Peter always loved the Salesians, and had always urged them to continue opening craft schools and agricultural schools throughout the country.

Peter was buried in St. John's Cemetery, Queens, in a grave given us by Fr. Pierre Conway, a Dominican. "Do not forget," Mary Frecon, head of our Harrisburg House, said before she left, "do not forget to tell of the roots of the little tree that they cut through in digging his grave. I kept looking at those roots and thinking how wonderful it is that Peter is going to nourish that tree, that thing of beauty." The undertaker tried to sell us artificial grass to cover up the soil, "the unsightly grave," as he called it, but we loved the sight of that earth that was to cover Peter. He had come up from the earth as we all had, and to the earth he was returning. Around the grave we all said the rosary, and after the Benedictus we left.

He was a man of sincerity and peace, and yet one letter came to us recently, accusing him of having a holier-than-thou attitude. Yes, Peter pointed out that it was a precept that we should love God with our whole heart and soul and mind and strength, and he taught us what it meant to be sons of God, and restored to us our sense of responsibility in a chaotic world. Yes, he was "holier than thou," holier than anyone we ever knew.

Peter Maurin died as he had lived the last twenty years of his life. He was laid to rest in a borrowed suit in a borrowed grave. In history's judgment his life and work had little significance. There is no movement named after him, his ideas are not mentioned in any general text of philosophy or religion, despite his numerous essays on both. He left nothing that we can objectively document as evidence of his success.

However, in his failure was Maurin's greatest triumph. He reminded us that true community, for which all humanity yearns, lies beyond temporal measurement. His Green Revolution was more than a simple "return-to-the-land" refrain. It called people to be at peace with each other and with the earth, to take no more than was needed, to share, to love, and to seek the harmony with earth and humanity that comes from envisioning the infinite.

In Maurin's mind, the nineteenth century, which nurtured the seemingly miraculous world of material progress, upset the balance between spiritual and material, and as a result it prefaced a century of unprecedented violence and crimes against the human community. Maurin wanted to rebalance the spiritual with the material. His model was Christ, the voice of God entering history in order to redeem it, the preeminent fusion of the infinite with the finite. For this reason, he literally "put on Christ," as Dorothy Day said. He loved, he shared, and he lived the beatitudes, in the never-dying hope of realizing the kingdom of God. He "so felt the tremendous importance of this life," Day wrote, "he made us feel the magnificent significance of our work, our daily lives, the material of God's universe, and what we did with it and how we used it." In *Loaves and Fishes* Dorothy offered this assessment of Peter:

> *He was good as bread. He was not gay or joyful, as others have described him, but he was a truly happy man, with the happiness a man feels when he has found his vocation in life and has set out on the way and is sure of himself: and sure, too, that others are searching for and willing to undertake their task in life, striving not only to love God and their brother but to show that love. Peter had faith in people as well as in ideas, and he was able to make them feel his faith in them, so that they gained confidence and overcame the sense of futility that so plagues the young of today. In fact, he gave me so great a faith in the power of his ideas that if he had said, "Go to Madison Square Garden and speak these ideas," I would have overcome all sense of fear and would have attempted such a folly, convinced that, though it was the "folly of the Cross" and doomed to failure, God Himself could take this failure and turn it into victory.*[1]

Maurin knew that the world could not live in a spiritual vacuum for long, and that there would be a new yearning for the divine. What to do with that desire became the essence of his message. By fixing his sight on eternity, Maurin affirmed that the world could become more like the true community of which we now only dream.

"We are gentle personalists," his followers used to say. "We will move people by our example; we will become what we want the other fellow to be." This was the message Peter Maurin left. He created a synthesis based on his faith, on his experiences, and his traditions, and he attempted to live that synthesis. In this way his simple life touched directly or indirectly a number of people who, through the Catholic Worker, created a voice for Catholic social justice where none had existed.

Maurin's death did not halt his "one-man revolution." Just as Maurin called Dorothy Day to a life of saintliness, his memory, his challenge to redeem the world through personal love and responsibility, calls us all. Dorothy recognized the need to write a biography of Maurin, for she realized that the story of his life offered a parable about how each person could live, in order to "make the future a little better than the past." And foster a society, as Maurin would say,

> Based on creed,
> not greed,
> on systematic unselfishness
> instead of systematic selfishness,
> on gentle personalism
> instead of rugged individualism,
> a new society [created]
> within the shell of the old.

Notes

Preface

1. David O'Brien, "The Pilgrimage of Dorothy Day," *Commonweal*, December 19, 1980, 711.
2. William Miller, *A Harsh and Dreadful Love: A History of the Catholic Worker Movement* (New York: Boni & Liveright, 1973); and William Miller, *Dorothy Day: A Biography* (San Francisco: Harper & Row, 1982).
3. Catholic Worker Archives, Marquette University, DD-CW, Series W-15, Box 2.
4. A recent movie about Dorothy Day, *Entertaining Angels*, confirms this view of Maurin. Martin Sheen portrays Maurin as a hard-to-understand eccentric foreigner who wanders in and out of the film for a little comic relief in what is otherwise a very good dramatic portrayal of Day and the Catholic Worker in its early years.
5. Marc H. Ellis, *Peter Maurin: Prophet in the Twentieth Century* (New York: Paulist Press, 1981), 16-18.
6. John Cogley, *A Canterbury Tale* (New York: Seabury, 1976), 10.
7. *The Dill Pickler* (Newberry Library manuscript collection "Dill Pickle Club"), 3.
8. Dorothy Day to Llewelyn Jones, Labor Day, 1927, Catholic Worker Archives, Marquette University, DD-CW, Series W-15, Box 2.

Introduction: Day and Maurin

1. Dorothy Day to Brendan O'Grady, June 2, 1954, Catholic Worker Archives, Marquette University, DD-CW, Series W-10, Box 1.
2. Dorothy Day to William Miller, January 1973, William Miller/Catholic Worker Archives, St. Thomas University, Miami, Florida, Box 1.
3. William Miller, *Dorothy Day: A Biography* (San Francisco: Harper & Row, 1982), xii.
4. Dorothy Day to William Miller, January 26, 1976, William Miller/Catholic Worker Archives, St. Thomas University, Miami, Florida, Box 1.
5. Cyril Echele to Arthur Sheehan, September 26, 1958, Catholic Worker Archives, Marquette University, DD-CW, Series W-15, Box 3.
6. Joseph Breig to Arthur Sheehan, August 25, 1958, Catholic Worker Archives, Marquette University, DD-CW, Series W-15, Box 3. Breig also related this story in an article in *Ave Maria* (January 20, 1962).

7. Dorothy Day, "Peter Maurin, A Biography," unpublished manuscript, William Miller/Catholic Worker Archives, St. Thomas University, Miami, Florida, Box 2 (hereafter: Day ms.).

8. Ibid., 27.

9. Dorothy Day, *The Long Loneliness* (New York: Harper & Brothers, 1952), 171.

10. Ibid.

11. Day ms., 40.

12. Ibid.

13. Peter Maurin, *Easy Essays* (Chicago: Franciscan Herald Press, 1977), 3.

14. Day ms., 136-37.

15. Ibid.

16. Ibid., 349.

17. Ibid., 167.

18. Day ms., 28.

19. Dorothy Day to Fr. Stanley Murphy, December 6, 1934, Catholic Worker Archives, Marquette University, DD-CW, Series W-10, Box 1.

20. Day ms., 13.

21. Ibid., 10-11.

22. Ibid., 12.

23. Antonio Gramsci, *An Antonio Gramsci Reader: Selected Writings 1916-1935*, ed. David Forgacs (New York: Schocken Books, 1988), 331.

24. Day ms., 26.

25. Ibid.

26. Ibid., 35-36.

27. Ibid., 37.

1. The French Peasant

1. Letter of Richard Louis, mayor of St. Julien du Tournel, to Arthur Sheehan, n.d., Catholic Worker Archives, Marquette University, DD-CW, Series W-15, Box 2.

2. Norbert Maurin to Arthur Sheehan, January 12, 1956, Catholic Worker Archives, Marquette University, DD-CW, Series W-15, Box 2.

3. Dorothy Day to Father McSorley, n.d. (circa 1933), Catholic Worker Archives, Marquette University, DD-CW, Series W-10, Box 1.

4. Author's visit to Oultet in June 2003.

5. Emmanuel Le Roy Ladurie, *The Peasants of Languedoc*, trans. John Day (Champagne: University of Illinois Press, 1977), 34.

6. Author interview with Arthur Sheehan, June 10, 1972. Arthur Sheehan, *Peter Maurin: Gay Believer* (Garden City, N.J.: Doubleday, 1959), 10.

7. Pierre de Coberton, *The Evolution of France under the Third Republic*, trans. Isabel Hapgood (New York: Thomas Crowell, 1897), 296-97.

8. Ibid.

9. Parker Thomas Moon, *The Labor Problem and the Social Movement in France: A Study in the History of Social Politics* (New York: Macmillan, 1921), 79.

10. Ibid., 83-85.

11. Ibid., 102-11.

12. Ibid., 115-17.

13. Dorothy Day, "Reflections on Work," *Catholic Worker*, January 1947.

14. Peter Maurin, *The Green Revolution: Easy Essays on Catholic Radicalism* (Chicago: Omega Graphics, 1976), 69.

15. Ibid., 18.

16. Albert Feuillerat, *French Life and Ideals,* trans. Vera Barbour (New Haven: Yale University Press, 1925), 113-14.

17. Visit to this area and interview with Jean Maurin, nephew of Peter Maurin, Oultet, France, June 17, 1998.

18. Letter from Angel Isidore, Visiteur General, Christian Brothers, Rome, to Brendan Anthony O'Grady, August, 23, 1952. Letter reprinted in Brendan Anthony O'Grady, "Peter Maurin, Propagandist" (dissertation, University of Ottawa, 1954).

19. Charles Breunig, "The Sillon of Marc Sangnier: Christian Democracy in France 1894-1910" (dissertation, Harvard University, 1953), 114.

20. Ibid.

21. Ibid., 116.

22. Ibid., 118.

23. Ibid., 125-27.

24. Ibid., 124.

25. Ibid.

26. Ibid., 119.

27. Maurin, *Green Revolution,* 99

28. Peter Maurin, "Christianity and Democracy," *The Catholic Worker,* January 1941, 1, 7.

29. Letter from Norbert Maurin to Arthur Sheehan, January 12, 1956, Catholic Worker Archives, Marquette University, DD-CW, Series W-15, Box 2.

2. Canada

1. Bob Weber, *Saskatchewan History Along the Highway* (Alberta, Canada: Red Dear College Press, 1998), 149.

2. Arthur Sheehan, *Peter Maurin: Gay Believer* (Garden City, N.J.: Doubleday, 1959), 72-73.

3. Herman Gangemoort, ed., *A Dutch Homesteader on the Prairies: The Letters of Willem de Gelder 1910-1913* (Toronto: University of Toronto Press, 1974), 4-9.

4. John H. Archer and Charles Koester, *Footprints in Time: A Sourcebook in the History of Saskatchewan* (Canada: House of Grant, 1965), 65.

5. Gangemoort, ed., *A Dutch Homesteader,* 4-9.

6. Weber, *Saskatchewan History,* 155.

7. Mackintosh, *Prairie Settlement,* 176.

8. Gangemoort, ed., *A Dutch Homesteader,* 14-15.

9. Ibid.

10. Ibid.

11. Ibid.

12. Sheehan, *Peter Maurin,* 78.

13. Gangemoort, ed., *A Dutch Homesteader,* 16.

14. F. A. Talbot, *The Making of a Great Canadian Railway* (London: Seeley, Service & Company, 1912), 238.

15. Ibid., 251.

16. Ibid., 257-58.

17. Sheehan, *Peter Maurin,* 73.

18. Norman Fergus Black, *Saskatchewan and the Old Northwest* (Regina, Sask.: Northwest Historical Co., 1913), 510.

19. Ibid.
20. Ibid., 221.
21. Ibid., 233.
22. Weber, *Saskatchewan History*, 243-44.
23. Ibid., 245.
24. Ibid.

3. A Fateful Meeting

1. Thomas Barry, "Peter Maurin" interview, Catholic Worker Archives, Marquette University, DD-CW, Series W-10, Box 1.
2. Joseph A. Breig, "Apostle on the Bum," *Commonweal*, April 29, 1938, 9-12.
3. Joseph Breig to Arthur Sheehan, August 25, 1958, Catholic Worker Archives, Marquette University, DD-CW, Series W-15, Box 3.
4. Ibid.
5. Marc Ellis, *Peter Maurin: Prophet in the Twentieth Century* (New York: Paulist Press, 1981), 171.
6. An analysis of Maurin's thought was not the purpose of Day's manuscript; therefore it is not central to this book. Marc Ellis, *Peter Maurin: Prophet in the Twentieth Century*, provides a very good analysis of Maurin's thought. Another good analysis of the radical idea of the Catholic Worker (which in essence is the radical idea of Peter Maurin) can be found in William Miller, *A Harsh and Dreadful Love: A History of the Catholic Worker Movement* (New York: Boni & Liveright, 1973).
7. Ibid., 7.
8. Ellis, *Peter Maurin*, 37.
9. Peter Maurin, *The Green Revolution: Easy Essays on Catholic Radicalism* (Chicago: Omega Graphics, 1976), 6.
10. John Moody to Dorothy Day, May, 21, 1949, Catholic Worker Archives, Marquette University, DD-CW, Series W-15, Box 4.

4. The Catholic Worker Begins

1. Dorothy Day, *Loaves and Fishes* (New York: Harper & Row, 1963; Maryknoll, N.Y.: Orbis Books, 1997), 97.
2. Dorothy Day, *The Long Loneliness* (New York: Harper & Brothers, 1952), 175.
3. Day is referring to Stanley Vishnewski, who arrived at the Catholic Worker as a young student in the thirties and continued to be a part of the movement until his death in 1979.
4. Arthur Ekirch, *Ideologues and Utopias: The Impact of the New Deal on American Thought* (Chicago: Quadrangle Books, 1969), 152.
5. John Hellman, *Emmanuel Mounier and the New Catholic Left 1930-1950* (Toronto: University of Toronto Press, 1981), 82.
6. Arthur Schlesinger, *The Coming of the New Deal* (Boston: Houghton Mifflin, 1959), 362-63.
7. Ibid.
8. John Cogley, "Pacifists," *Commonweal*, October 23, 1953, 54.
9. James J. Farrell, *The Spirit of the Sixties: The Making of Post War Radicalism* (New York: Routledge Press, 1997), 14.

5. Life with Peter

1. An opera by Christoph Willibald Gluck, composed in 1767.

6. Clarification of Thought

1. Dorothy Day, *The Long Loneliness* (New York: Harper & Brothers, 1952), 220.

8. The Green Revolution

1. Emmanuel Mounier, *Personalism* (South Bend, Ind.: University of Notre Dame Press, 1952), 4-12.

2. Peter Maurin, *The Green Revolution: Essays on Catholic Radicalism* (Chicago: Omega Graphics, 1976), 39.

3. Donald Worster, "Transformations of the Earth: Toward an Agroecological Perspective in History," *The Journal of American History* 76, no. 4 (1990): 1090. This entire article provides an excellent review of current historical interest in the environment and the changes brought to it by human activity. For contemporary comments by environmentalists on a sustainable economy, see Thomas Berry, *The Dream of the Earth* (San Francisco: Sierra Book Club, 1988), esp. chap. 7; see also Lester Brown, "Picturing a Sustainable Society," *The Elmwood Newsletter* 6 (spring, 1990): 1, 4, 10.

4. Wayne Morgan, "Populism and Agriculture," in H. Wayne Morgan, *The Gilded Age* (Syracuse, N.Y.: Syracuse University Press, 1971), 170.

5. Worster, "Transformations of the Earth," 1100.

6. Ibid., 1105-6.

7. John Hugo, "'Capitalism Impractical,' a Defense of the Catholic Worker Commune," *Catholic Worker*, November 1939, 8.

8. Quoted in Worster, "Transformations of the Earth," 1100.

9. E. F. Schumacher, *Small is Beautiful: Economics as if People Mattered* (New York: Harper & Row, 1973), 23-39, 77-78.

10. *Catholic Worker*, September 1937, 1, 8; also Marc Ellis, *Peter Maurin: Prophet in the Twentieth Century* (New York: Paulist Press, 1981), 125-26.

11. Dorothy Day, "Farm Commune," *Catholic Worker*, November 1938, 8.

9. Peter's Digests

1. The papers to which Day is referring were handwritten by Maurin and are preserved in the Catholic Worker Archives at Marquette University.

10. A Good Man

1. Dorothy Day, *Loaves and Fishes* (New York: Harper & Row, 1963; Maryknoll, N.Y.: Orbis Books, 1997), 10.

Acknowledgments

Jacques Barzun said that a student of cultural history is the last person who can claim to be self-made or the sole begetter of his or her most original idea. With that in mind, I am happy to acknowledge at least some of the intellectual and spiritual debt I accumulated in the creation of this work. First of all I am grateful to Emma Lapsansky, director of a National Endowment for the Humanities Summer Institute on Religion and Diversity, at Haverford College, and to my fellow participants, who nudged me in the direction of this project. The following year, the NEH also provided funds for a summer seminar at the Newberry Library in Chicago, where much of the preliminary research for this work was done. There is no finer place to work than the Newberry and no finer group of scholars with whom to share ideas. I am particularly grateful to Elliot Gorn of the Newberry, who helped me to conceptualize what form this book might take.

I spent time in Peter Maurin's village in Southern France, breathing the air, and visiting the places he knew so well as a child. For the privilege of this experience I am grateful to the Maurin family of Oultet, especially Jean Baptist Maurin, Peter's great nephew, who took me into his home (which was once Peter's) and shared a cup of Pernod, stories about life in his mountaintop village, and memories of his famous uncle. Until recently they still received the *Catholic Worker,* which mysteriously began arriving in the early 1940s. I am also grateful to the people at the Marquette University Archives, particularly Phil Runkel, whose mastery of the Catholic Worker papers ensures that time spent at "the Chives," as he calls it, is always well spent.

I am also grateful to our own archivist, Margaret Elliston, who as our former library director was instrumental in bringing the William Miller/ Catholic Worker papers to our library. St. Thomas University has been my academic home since I started teaching, and it is a good place to work. Not all small colleges appreciate the scholarly side of academic life, but the administration at St. Thomas does. They kept committee demands to a minimum, provided me with a sabbatical, a summer research grant, and a clean, quiet place to work. What else is needed? The interdisciplinary mix of our small college provided a sense of community and exchange of ideas that has been especially helpful to me. I am particularly grateful to my colleagues— Richard Raleigh, Jim Conley, Helen Jacobstein, Gloria Ruiz, Tom Ryan, Jorge Sardiñas, Terry Veling, Gary Feinberg, Andrea Campbell, Elizabeth Ferrero, Jim MacDougall, and Ruben Arango—who through their intelligence and insights have helped me to think through my own ideas more carefully. I am especially thankful for the friendship of Joe Holland of our philosophy department, who helped me flesh out ideas on Catholic social thought that were fundamental to Maurin's synthesis, and whose insight, encouragement, and good humor helped keep me going through those tough but creative times of self-doubt.

My association over the years with the American Catholic Historical Association has also been of great benefit. It was at ACHA meetings where many of the ideas in this book were first presented, and the comments from colleagues at these conferences have become part of the final product. I am particularly grateful to Anne Klejment, whose insight into Dorothy Day's personality helped me greatly as I tried to clarify Dorothy's thoughts on Peter. A special word of gratitude is also due to the editor-in-chief at Orbis, Robert Ellsberg. As former editor of the *Catholic Worker,* his intimate knowledge of the movement and his keen editorial eye brought this work to a much better place than it ever could have been without him.

And I will always be grateful to Bill Miller and Rhea Bond Miller, who in my younger years shared with me their hospitality, their intelligence, their family, and their vision of the scholarly life, which I too, partly as a result of their influence, have chosen. And finally, to my wife, Isabel, who shared and supported this journey with fluent French, suggestions, humor, encouragement, but most of all love.